PARSONAGE AND PARSON

A winsome, witty, and often poignant book. *Parsonage and Parson* offers an inside view of a period when the Anglican parish was undergoing a historic shift – away from a centuries-old pattern of rambling rectories and often eccentric arrangements to a Church of England that was more professionalised, but somehow less assured of its place in the landscape. These reminiscences of a Diocesan estate manager – often hilarious, sometimes grievous - are told with much affection for this ancient institution and those who faithfully serve it, providing a valuable commentary on what we have both lost and retained.

Rt Rev'd Dr Andrew Rumsey, Bishop of Ramsbury.
Author of the acclaimed pastoral journal 'English Grounds'.

PARSONAGE AND PARSON

Coping with the Clergy – Thirty years
of eccentricity and delight

RICHARD TRAHAIR

The Book Guild Ltd

First published in Great Britain in 2022 by
The Book Guild Ltd
Unit E2 Airfield Business Park,
Harrison Road, Market Harborough,
Leicestershire. LE16 7UL
Tel: 0116 2792299
www.bookguild.co.uk
Email: info@bookguild.co.uk
Twitter: @bookguild

Copyright © 2022 Richard Trahair

The right of Richard Trahair to be identified as the author of this
work has been asserted by them in accordance with the
Copyright, Design and Patents Act 1988.

All rights reserved. No part of this publication may be
reproduced, transmitted, or stored in a retrieval system, in any form or by any means,
without permission in writing from the publisher, nor be otherwise circulated in
any form of binding or cover other than that in which it is published and without
a similar condition being imposed on the subsequent purchaser.

This work is entirely fictitious and bears no resemblance to any persons living or dead.

Typeset in 11pt Minion Pro

Printed and bound in the UK by TJ Books LTD, Padstow, Cornwall

ISBN 978 1915122 933

British Library Cataloguing in Publication Data.
A catalogue record for this book is available from the British Library.

Dedicated in memory of the late Rt Rev John Neale AKC, my mentor and guide through the undergrowth of the Church of England.

INTRODUCTION
WHATEVER IS A PARSONAGE?

(The reader may wish to skip this if already familiar with Church machinery – or anxious to avoid it.)

'Parsonage' is the correct name for the house provided in the Church of England for the occupation of a person appointed for the 'cure of souls' within a 'benefice', a geographical parish or group of parishes that, in total, cover the entire landmass of England. (Well, some are partially submerged underwater at high tide in coastal regions or indeed flooded by bursting riverbanks inland.)

A benefice will have been either a 'rectory' or a 'vicarage'. These terms refer to the nature of the post, not the accommodation. Oh, what Anglican pride and prejudice has been generated over the years by parishioners of rectories over their lesser mortals in deprived neighbouring benefices that are merely vicarages. This one-upmanship has unfortunately come to be manifest simply in the nameplate on the gate of the parsonage, these days, of which more anon.

Originally, all benefices were rectories. The rector was often an absentee (notoriously exemplified in Trollope's *The Warden* by the incumbent holder of a benefice choosing to reside in Italy).

Absentees or overworked rectors would then appoint a vicar to serve in the parish vicariously on behalf of the rector, or in addition to him.

Over the centuries, such benefices will have been divided up or united and eventually many have ended up solely as vicarages.

To further complicate matters, increasingly in recent decades, the benefices have been formally retained by the bishop, who has then appointed priests-in-charge to run them for him.[1] Why, one might ask.

So here we come to the nub of the story and the motivation for so many characters in this book to behave in the way that I relate from more than thirty years' experience as Diocesan Property Secretary and Secretary to the Parsonages Board for a large diocese in the South of England, in secular parlance part of my duties as the estate manager for land and property extending over five counties of England.

---

[1] For most of my career, parish clergy were only male and most of the anecdotes which follow relate to clergy of that ilk. These days the prevalence of wonderful women priests has introduced into the Church an aura of calm sanity in its pastoral life in which the incidents described could surely never have occurred?

WHATEVER IS A PARSONAGE?

This crucial distinction, unique to the Church of England, is that incumbent rectors and vicars have the titular right to the *freehold* of their house, whereas priests-in-charge merely hold a (withdrawable) licence from the bishop. One of the justifications for the freehold of incumbents was the independence this gave them to promote the Gospel and serve the people without fear or favour from the people. This, of course, was anathema to bishops, who understandably wished to exercise some basic control over what their parsons were up to. Hence the modern practice of 'suspension of presentation to the living' (i.e. preventing ecclesiastical patrons from appointing incumbents to the freehold) and putting in a priest on licence instead so that the bishop can exert some measure of influence over the wilder eccentricities of his clergy that would otherwise have flourished rampantly in the ways which I will go on to describe.

Today, these distinctions have lost their impact. Secular legislation on the workplace has filtered through to the Church of England, and the relationship between parish clergy and bishop has become more collegiate, more consultative– and more prescriptive.

It is only amongst parishioners that the old distinctions are still observed. In my time I would religiously arrange for the house signs to be changed from 'rectory' to 'vicarage' or vice versa, if pastoral reorganisation altered the title of the post. This practice did not go down well in the parish that had been a rectory and was now subjugated to a supposedly inferior status.

In all too many cases, benefices have been combined, one or other of their parsonages becoming redundant in consequence. (The legal term is 'united', but in my experience unity between the parishioners of each formerly independent benefice was rarely a feature of enforced life together. Pity the poor parson. Herding cats was a cinch in comparison with his[1] uphill struggle.)

Even more controversial, especially in the eyes of London-based journalists writing for expensive magazines devoted to the urban myth of rural living, was the practice of replacing large, grand old parsonages with more compact modern homes. This was part of my duties, under direction of course from the boards and committees concerned; one which I was obliged to carry out extensively during the 1980s and 1990s, often with chagrin and a sense of loss and sometimes with little practical justification.

There were four substantive reasons for selling large period parsonages and replacing them with smaller family homes.

Clergy on survival stipends have not the means to heat, decorate or furnish them, nor maintain the often extensive grounds. They and their families should not have to shiver indoors in winter nor devote their summers to cutting the grass.

Old parsonages are part of an important national heritage and history, but the Church is severely under-resourced to maintain them to conservation standard or provide the level of comfort expected in modern society.

A diocese has the duty to house its clergy and their families in economical comfort and adequate privacy. Ideally, the new houses should be purpose-designed and built to the C of E 'Green Guide' standard regardless of the location, be it a wealthy, leafy benefice in Sussex or a concrete, graffitied ghetto of deprivation anywhere else. Hence the commitment in my time to build parsonages with what was then the forefront of technology, such as ground source heating, use of solar gain, grey water recycling, inbuilt fire sprinkler systems and triple glazing.

Underlying these practical reasons is the far deeper philosophical and doctrinal centrality of our theological raison d'être, all too rarely expressed in the context of the parsonage house. Since the end of World War I the Church has sought to identify itself with the interests of the poor, the underprivileged and the downtrodden to an articulate degree that was unimaginable during the heyday of the grand old parsonage, with the assumptions of the parson who resided in them as well as 'the poor man at the gate'; a lengthy period in which both high and lowly took it for granted that God had ordered their estate. The established Church of England has a way to go yet, in this regard.

So, there are four reasons. There is a fifth, bringing us back down to earth with a bump. This one is unlikely to feature as part of any consultative presentation to a parochial church council (PCC) by diocesan officers hoping to minimise local opposition to the loss of its dearly loved parsonage.

To survive as a going concern, a diocese needs both capital and income. Income is of course generated mainly through parish or deanery 'share' or 'quota', largely to maintain clergy training, ministry and accommodation.

But no organisation can survive at a standstill. It moves either forwards or backwards. 'Forwards' means responding to the need for a Church presence on a huge new housing estate; building a place of worship; building or buying accommodation for a priest; providing a loan or grant fund for parishes to help restore their parish churches; purchasing homes for assistant curates appointed for the first time in busy, overworked parishes; or ploughing into a diocesan reserve fund to help during times of income crisis such as global pandemics.

Where can this capital be found? Long gone are the automatic capital grants from the Church Commissioners of the 1970s and '80s. There is only one easily realisable source of capital available now – the sale proceeds of a redundant parsonage or the surplus arising from a parsonage replacement. (I will come to Diocesan 'glebe' later.)

We try not to mention this anywhere outside the Diocesan Office.

At any rate, so many of these architectural gems (and a few monstrosities) had to go. In the 1980s, I was selling them at the rate of one every couple of months. The 1970s had been even worse, perhaps borne along by the 'Brave New World' attitude of that decade. Unfortunately, that new world did not extend to high-quality softwood timber or reliable Chinese copper piping imports and did insist on huge, single-glazed windows. As a result, the hideously ugly new parsonages constructed in the '70s caused far more maintenance headaches and expense than their eighteenth- and nineteenth-century predecessors would have done.

Until the late '80s, the Church Commissioners required all parsonage sales to be by public auction, presumably as the best means of demonstrating institutional honesty and corporate transparency. Those auctions were great fun, held locally to the property in question and attended by the diocesan solicitor and me, to answer last-minute questions and receive mutterings and worse from certain locals in the back row who should have known better. (See the first example of parsonical behaviour in due course.)

Demand for these old houses had picked up by the early '80s, and we could always be confident of a healthy attendance of bidders. I recall only one case where the offering was withdrawn with no bids above reserve following those plucked off the back wall by the auctioneer. In that instance we sold at the reserve plus a bit, to a late bidder after the auction room had emptied.

Back in the 1960s, old parsonages had been virtually unsaleable, by auction or otherwise. No one was interested, and many houses had lain empty and neglected for years.

But business was booming in the '80s. My (fifteenth-century) office had rows of sales particulars' photographs lined around the ceiling cornice as decorative scalps. I tried to find them the other day, in the box I had put in the Diocesan Office attic forty years ago, but it was long gone.

Redundant parsonages were never allowed to be marketed with a name that might imply they were, or could remain, an official clergy house. (Only on one occasion ever did the bishop permit a retiring incumbent vicar to purchase his parsonage and go on living there. The vicar's retirement had coincided with local benefice reorganisation that rendered his house redundant.)

Houses therefore had to be sold as 'the former parsonage/rectory/vicarage and never as 'The Old Rectory' or 'The Old Vicarage'. There was a good practical reason for this. If the new owners chose another name, they would be spared endless confusion by the postman and unwelcome visits by the regular tramps calling at the door for a cup of tea and a sandwich.

Needless to say, few purchasers ever resisted the temptation, and in the week after completion of a sale, one could always anticipate a smart new nameplate appearing on the gate proudly proclaiming: 'The Old Rectory'.

Occasionally I would forget to prise off 'The Rectory' sign before the sale, and there are several private families still living in houses purporting to be a benefice parsonage because they have never got around to removing it themselves.

It is undeniable that even in these secular times when the Church no longer holds key position in high society, living in 'The Old Rectory' or 'The Old Vicarage' – or even 'The Former Parsonage' as one literalist purchaser adopted – holds considerable panache. I should mention for the sake of completeness, that there are two further parochial clergy posts for which the diocese provides accommodation. One is the Assistant Curacy (a kind of ecclesiastical apprenticeship), and the other is that noble position held by an experienced priest, which is entirely unpaid but provides a house free of rent, council tax and rates in return for several days' pastoral duty a week.

Odd, isn't it, that one never hears new owners calling their home 'The Old Assistant Curacy'? And what about 'The Old House-for-Duty'? We will move on.

ONE

WHO LOOKS AFTER THE PARSONAGES AND KEEPS AN EYE ON THE OCCUPANTS?

I joined the diocesan staff as a twenty-nine-year-old chartered surveyor to the post of Secretary to the Diocesan Parsonages Board, Secretary to the Diocesan Glebe Committee and Deputy Diocesan Secretary. I had a necessarily elongated brass plate to that effect on my office door.

I had succeeded a retired army brigadier who had died suddenly in unfortunate circumstances, and I obtained the job largely because I was not the chartered engineer which the job advertisements had inexplicably specified. My two fellow candidates on interview day were both engineers and were wholly mystified by the total absence of any engineering aspect to the post concerned.

What the role required was a good old land agent, well accustomed to managing grand mansions inhabited by elderly eccentrics and surrounded by acres of neglected pasture. Well, they got a land agent but not one 'over forty years of age' as mooted in the advertisement.

In those days, diocesan administration was a skeleton affair. There were four executives, each with a typist secretary, no accountant (only a bookkeeper) and no vast Safeguarding and Wellbeing Control Industry Department such as rules the roost today in order to protect the institution's reputation.

The Diocesan Board and its staff contained a group captain as Chairman, naval captain as Vice Chairman, a rear admiral, a cavalry half-colonel who wore a monocle (my boss, a delightful man), a long-suffering squadron leader, a somewhat disinterested major from a famous tank regiment and me. (I had been merely a lance corporal in my school CCF.)

This set-up was presumably what Cranmer had in mind in the *Book of Common Prayer* when praying for 'the whole state of Christ's Church Militant here in Earth'.

There were about twelve of us in total, including a peak-capped porter who lived in the porter's lodge by the office courtyard entrance and whose principal responsibility was to empty the wastepaper baskets and prevent visiting octogenarian members of the ecclesiastical reading room from scraping their cars against the fifteenth-century stonework on their way in and out of the private car park.

The rest of us rattled around the ground floor of a range of buildings dating from that century through to Victorian that had been the city workhouse until acquired in the 1880s as the first Diocesan Office in England *(Fig.1)*.

My boss's office had been the workhouse lock-up and still contained an ancient privy now devoted to storing back copies of the pre-war *Diocesan Gazette* and spare carbon paper.

Upstairs was the board room, a medieval solar still with its fifteenth-century fireplace. The rest of the first floor was empty, occasionally being hired out for grade examinations on the resident upright piano. Those in the office beneath grew accustomed to the repeated strains of 'Für Elise' endlessly tinkling from overhead. A disused and dusty chapel at the far end was the stationery cupboard, lit by sunlight through the faded colours of its stained-glass windows.

Fig. 1

My previous job had been as a junior land agent with Strutt and Parker, based on the other side of the city. I don't think that the office culture at S&P had been particularly progressive, but my accustomed practice there proved to ruffle the feathers of the Diocesan Office to a significant extent. For one thing, I started dictating letters and papers on a desktop cassette tape dictating machine that I found in its original unopened box in a cupboard. My secretary was aghast. For twenty years she had begun the day taking shorthand from my predecessor's verbal dictation, typing drafts and then producing fair copy for him to sign at the end of the day.

We quickly had to borrow another member of staff who could use a headset and playback machine.

What really caused a stir, however, was my unthinking habit of addressing, and referring to, colleagues by their Christian names. This was unheard of. The colonel and the squadron leader had to hold an emergency meeting to define acceptable practice. My influence bore fruit, but there were still one or two mature secretaries of long-standing who, twenty years later, were still addressing their superiors by their surnames and military ranks.

In those days, the bishop had his office in the same building. He was a generous, outgoing character who ought really to have been a theatre actor. He had the disconcerting habit of putting his head round my office door unannounced and asking some arcane technical question for illustrative purposes in his next sermon.

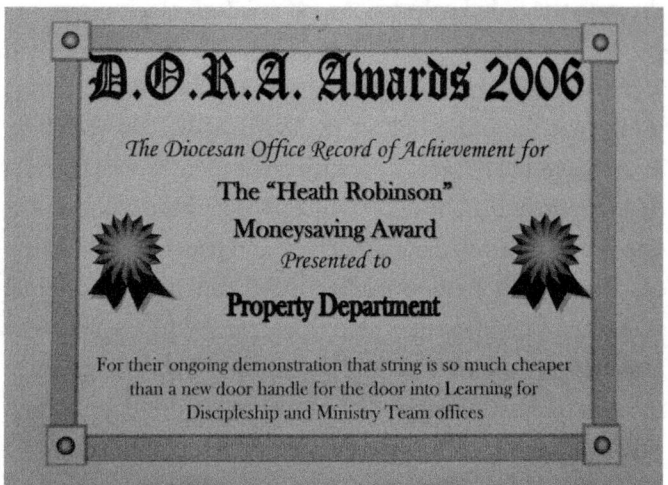

Fig. 2

He it was who, on welcoming me to my new job, cautioned me most firmly not to stay for more than five years, otherwise (as he put it) 'the army council is bound to get you down'. I overran his timescale by more than a factor of six but never regretted it until the last few years when secular corporatism and dreadful IT finally swamped all that remained of the spirit of pastoral Christian amateur professionalism that had created and sustained the Diocesan Office community with such faithful commitment and much fun and laughter (*Fig. 2*) for so many years.

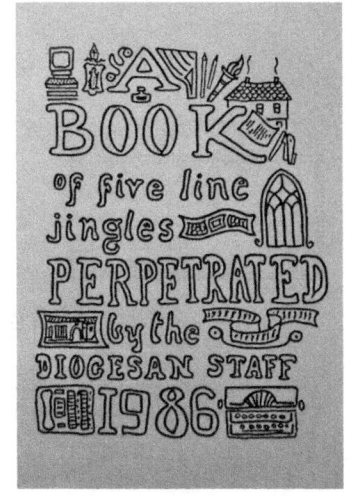

Fig. 3

Gone with the turn of the millennium were the office limerick competitions (*Fig. 3*) judged by a suffragan bishop; the staff choral concerts offering disgraceful Noël Coward adaptations (the stately Church of England…); and the full-length scripted slide show film *Down at the Workhouse* which mercilessly lampooned every attempt to haul the Church of England administration into the twentieth century. Somehow, the Diocesan Office had lost its sense of humour, and I was happy to leave it.

TWO
ECCENTRIC PARSONAGE HOUSES?

But now, back to the glory days of the early 1980s. I will try to present a series of snapshots of a few of my parsonage houses (out of the then total of 240) and their occupants that made my professional life so fascinating.

I shall set out my samples in correct archidiaconal order, from south-west to north-east. Some will be readily believable; others will be less so. All are true, but to avoid aggrieving friends and relations and to prevent any slight risk of libel, I am not identifying individuals by anything other than title, their actual names known only to myself and my solicitor.

I have been uncertain what to do about place names. Date and place would very easily serve to identify the people concerned, and so with reluctance, I must forego the names of towns and villages.

ECCENTRIC PARSONAGE HOUSES?

This chapter concerns the houses themselves and their often curious demesnes.

I begin in the far south-west, a regency seaside parish of Holy Trinity. The parsonage was mid-nineteenth century, a tall gaunt building with narrow lancet windows and a slightly creepy ambiance reminiscent of old Hammer films. It was cold and perpetually wet from porous stonework saturated by westerly storms. The assistant curate lived in the garden, in the former carriage house that had been converted in the 1950s to basic domestic accommodation largely comprising soggy fibreboard. The extensive grounds were surrounded by a high stone wall topped with one or two remaining tile capstones, barbed wire and shards of glass embedded in mortar. Clearly an earlier incumbent had not been keen on unannounced visitors.

The arrangement was adequate except for the unfortunate fact that in my early days the vicar and the curate had ceased speaking to each other. This made mutual gardening co-operation difficult.

*

We next move along the coast westwards to a very pretty picture-postcard village of thatched cottages and warm stone, close to a popular pebble beach excellent for bathing. The rectory is one of the gems and remains a parsonage house to this day. It possesses a square, flat lawn precisely the right size for a tennis court, a couple of magnificent ancient spreading trees and a range of outbuildings that include a small domestic conversion which I sold off to raise maintenance funds. The large rambling house itself is essentially eighteenth/nineteenth century and hardly eccentric, except for one astonishing feature. The principal rooms face a lawn alongside a narrow minor lane running down to a boundary wall that has a garden door at low level into the old kitchen garden. This was for the use of domestic servants.

Fig. 4

However, the kitchen quarters were at the opposite end of the house. How to enjoy the outlook from the drawing room without one's view being despoiled by the lower servant classes passing to and fro before one's eyes? Well, the then rector had a brilliant idea. He had a stone– and brick-lined tunnel dug beneath the lawns connecting the lower ground floor of the kitchen quarters with the vegetable garden behind the bank in the south-west corner of the pleasure grounds. By this means, the lesser mortals could scurry back and forth underground while the rector and his family gazed out unimpeded. The tunnel is still there (*Fig. 4*) but these days a hard hat would be prudent beyond the steel bars of the door.

*

ECCENTRIC PARSONAGE HOUSES?

Moving inland now to an ancient episcopal town and its unsurpassed abbey church, we find the solid, dignified vicarage standing in the close at the church's west end, a kind of would-be deanery, occupied by a long succession of clerics who comported themselves like cathedral deans and with some justification. Over the close wall to the north lies the venerable public school in all its brown stone glory. I attended that place of learning in the mid-1960s and am tempted to go off here on a diversion about even greater eccentric characters, but no, I will stick to my theme. The unusual feature of this vicarage (before part of the house was divided off as an independent let flat) was its first-floor landing corridor. It was precisely twenty-two yards long, and I well remember, in the days of my youth, practising my batting and bowling as a short-sighted fourteen-year-old. The canon drew the line at us using a cricket ball, as there was a rather fine tall window behind the stumps, so we had to use a soft squashy one borrowed from his dog.

*

A little further north in a feudal village stands a truly magnificent rectory of immense proportions, its original garden frontage being twice as long as any other seventeenth- or eighteenth-century parsonage in the diocese. Indeed, it could quite reasonably be described as a palace, because at one time it was the gracious residence of the former Archbishop of Canterbury, Dr Fisher. At some point before my time, however, this stately home was divided in two, including the grounds, and one half sold off.

PARSONAGE AND PARSON

My good friend Canon Henry was rector there for many years and took great delight in telling people that he just lived in a 'semi'. Most 'semis' could easily fit inside his high-ceilinged kitchen.

*

We then move across two counties north-eastwards to an old red-brick village in the New Forest. Here was an elegant vicarage set up on its own bit of rising ground and reached by a curving gravel drive lined with laurel bushes. The parish church was immediately adjacent. Unique in the diocese, and quite possibly anywhere else, was that the parish still employed a church verger (a sort of liturgical foreman and maintenance man) living with his wife in the ancient verger's cottage at the bottom of the garden, still owned by the diocese. Both the verger and his wife were very advanced in years but far from advanced in their understanding or acceptance of any kind of modern convenience. The cottage was very pretty and its garden kept abundant with flowers and vegetables. A 'sentry box' privy (*Fig. 5*) stood in one corner of the garden,

Fig. 5

itself equally enchanting with ivy and honeysuckle growing all over it. The cottage had electricity but no plumbing or heating. There was an outside tap, and the aged couple drew water from it for the stone sink in the kitchen which served all their needs.

The verger's wife became very lame and frail, and social services began to take an interest. Our glebe agent and I decided that, as landlord, the diocese would do well to renew its encouragement to the elderly couple to accept some serious interior improvements, such as running hot water and some storage heaters. They would not hear of it. In the end, we did succeed in installing a bath, but they declined the nuisance of putting in plumbing and, for a while, tried a little hot water in the bath via a bucket from the tiny boiler behind the solid fuel Rayburn. However, in the end, they used the new bath for storing logs and reverted to the stone sink for their accustomed hygienic purposes.

*

From there I now take the reader about forty miles further north-west to a market town and its famous Long Street (the most elongated row of listed buildings in England). The distinguished eighteenth-century rectory stood off the pavement halfway down. It had a small space off the road for a small car, but visitors had to walk. The accommodation was laid out into classically proportioned principal rooms but had one rather awkward bottleneck. The only door into the rear garden opened directly out of the ground-floor lavatory, which made summer alfresco parish entertaining a potentially embarrassing business, requiring careful management. Sadly,

I had to sell the place eventually, but not before the buyer's surveyor had noticed major subsidence at the edge of the rear lawn. On investigation with a spade, I discovered a huge crater opening up into a deep, dark cavity beneath my feet. A local archaeologist took an interest and found a brick-lined cellar with what appeared to be an underground passage back towards the house. The buyer was delighted. After good competitive market interest, the property sold well ahead of the agent's valuation for about £650,000. This was the only instance in which I ever came up against the naive expectations of an esoteric pressure group calling itself 'Save Our Parsonages'; a group of metro-romantics with decidedly rose-tinted views of what the Church of England ought to be but, in reality, had not been since about 1953. They also had London-centric opinions of what rural parsonages were worth, in this particular case insisting on the mind-boggling sum of £2 million. I offered to get another independent valuation, but this was ignored. They preferred to live with their fantasies.

*

Finally in this collection of building oddities, a little piece of historical rating law that is scarcely remembered these days. The relatively modern parsonage up in the north of the diocese was sold in about 1967. The buyer insisted on purchasing a long leasehold rather than the freehold. Surely a curious choice? But he was a canny individual and knew his rating legislation. A long time previously, someone in the diocese of Salisbury had won a rating tribunal case arguing that the rateable value (then used for domestic and water rates payable to the local council) of parsonages should be one third of that for equivalent private houses, because their rental value (the basis of RV) as tied accommodation for priests was that much lower. This decision came to be known as the 'Salisbury Judgment' and was applicable throughout the country. The clever buyer of the parsonage lease continued to enjoy a sixty-six per cent reduction in rates right through to their abolition under Margaret Thatcher and replacement with her 'poll tax', and now council tax. However, parsonages still retained their low RVs, and since this remains the basis for water rates, I always refused to allow my parsonages to have water meters installed instead. We must have saved hundreds of thousands of pounds over the decades.

THREE
THE PARSONS. SURELY A BREED APART?

In retrospect, and now being familiar with modern clergy who are more or less like the rest of us, I find it hard to believe that the stories which follow can possibly be true. However, I must assure my readers that these are factually accurate anecdotes of events and behaviour that I personally witnessed or at least had to mop up afterwards.

A little additional background will help to set the scene.

During the era I am describing, parish clergy were not obliged to retire at any particular age. The limit of seventy years was imposed a little later. Very many parsons continued in their (freehold) post until they were either carried out of the parsonage horizontally or in aged infirmity rescued by their family. Most had little choice. Their stipend was barely enough to live on, and in those days, there was wholly inadequate provision for pensions or retirement accommodation. (This provision, run by the Church of England Pensions Board, was soon to be dramatically transformed into an excellent system linking affordable rented bungalows to the retired parsons' much improved pension income.)

To add insult to injury, in 1978 the controversial Endowments and Glebe Measure 1976 came into force, finally removing the rights of individual incumbents to manage their own glebe. Glebe property and its income were transferred to the diocese for a more even distribution towards the remuneration of all its clergy. This was the ultimate step in a process that had gradually taken away an incumbent's entitlement to the income attached to his own particular benefice. Those who had enjoyed a large income from substantial historic glebe holdings loudly complained of this institutional theft. Those whose glebe property consisted of one small, waterlogged field kept very quiet.

The contrast that had existed between wealthy benefices and poor ones (another feature of Anthony Trollope's novels) was immense. Even in my time, a tiny rural benefice possessed as glebe two entire streets in South London, with a combined rental income that as long ago as 1911 had put a five-figure sum annually into the pocket of the parson.

What remained of this London bounty in 1981 had become something of an embarrassment. My Glebe Committee Chairman (the suffragan bishop) had decided to go and have a look and discovered from conversation with our London letting agent, and from his own observation, that the remaining glebe terraced houses were firmly in a notorious 'red light' district. The rental income unsurprisingly fluctuated as a result, and management had become such a headache that we decided to be shot of it, selling the let freeholds en bloc to a property investment company with less of a moral reputation to uphold than we had.

*

My first personal example of parsonical behaviour owes more to a fierce independence as freeholder than it does to eccentricity. The vicar was incumbent of a parish with a large parsonage house dating back to the sixteenth century in parts. Unfortunately, those parts were rapidly beginning to fall away from the rest of the structure, and we decided that it was no longer safe. The vicar refused to sell, and since it was his titular right to sign a conveyance, there was a stalemate. Eventually, the bishop persuaded him that if he moved out, he could continue in post and live in a small house in the same village which he had already (contrary to Church standing orders) purchased for his retirement.

This was to prove a strategic error on the bishop's part. The vicar verbally agreed and moved out of the vicarage. I duly arranged an auction sale in a nearby town and turned up with our solicitor and the auctioneer. The room was full, and bidding was brisk. Suddenly from the back of the room a loud voice arose, which halted the proceedings. The white-haired and black-coated figure of the vicar had stood up. For several minutes he harangued me, the auctioneer, the bishop and at least one churchwarden for depriving him of his vicarage and charged the archdeacon with blackmail and deception. With that he strode from the room and the bidding resumed. Somehow or other, the powers-that-be persuaded him to sign the conveyance a few weeks later, but that was by no means the end of the affair.

The parson chose to retire shortly afterwards and of course continued to live in his own cottage in the village. His successor was duly appointed, and in the meantime, we had built a smart new vicarage in the grounds of the old house, where we had retained a plot for that purpose. (The old crumbling parsonage had been bought by a glamorous fake countess from Eastern Europe somewhere.)

So now there were the new Vicar A and the retired Vicar B, both living cheek by jowl. The new vicar wrote up the parish magazine and despatched it to the local printer by a small boy on a bicycle. On several occasions what came back printed clearly differed in some respects from what had been drafted, but the crunch came with one edition which now included a colourful paragraph condemning the archdeacon and all his works in no uncertain terms.

It transpired that Vicar B had been intercepting the boy on the bicycle and redrafting the parish magazine before it resumed its journey to the printers.

I seem to remember that the archdeacon actually sued him for libel but I forget the eventual outcome.

I hope you are beginning to see some justification for the title of this book.

*

A brief interlude now, to visit the rectory in a county town, a modest nineteenth-century edifice of two stories overlooking the parish church on the other side of the road.

The rector lived on the first floor, having created for himself a makeshift flat upstairs. A jovial fellow, and warm-hearted, dearly loved by his parishioners, he had generously made over the entire ground floor as a parish hall and office for use by his parish secretary and the PCC – parochial church council – and indeed anyone else who wished to use it. We built a new parsonage in the orchard next to the house, and when the rector resigned the benefice, we sold his house. I remember little about this particular sale except for the vast quantity of empty bottles littered over the empty ground floor of the premises, bottles that had clearly at one time contained corks.

*

In the centre of the county was a small, undistinguished village, with an equally boring 1970's parsonage. The rector was one of those nervy, complaining types, always on the phone to the Diocesan Property Office with some niggle or other requiring attention. One morning, we received a call from him to say that a first-floor bedroom joist had cracked beneath the floorboards, and the ceiling below was beginning to split rather alarmingly. My immediate reaction, in light of previous experience with this individual, was 'oh yeah'; I would look into the matter in due course.

An hour later he phoned again to say that the ground-floor ceiling in the dining room had now collapsed onto the carpet in small pieces, and so I rang the surveyor for that archdeaconry to go and see what was up.

THE PARSONS. SURELY A BREED APART?

That afternoon the surveyor telephoned, scarcely able to contain his mirth. Apparently, the rector's wife (who had often complained about the small room sizes) had hired a hydraulic Kango hammer and had attacked the load-bearing block wall between dining and living rooms, having decided that the two rooms would be much better if combined into one. She had almost achieved her object when the weight of bedroom furniture overhead had caused the unforeseen difficulty earlier reported to me by her husband in terms which had implied that, somehow, it was all the fault of the diocese, a common default position adopted by difficult clergy to this day.

*

Along the south coast on an exquisite island (not actually an island but regarded as such by its residents, who would have quite liked a drawbridge) lay a village, sitting up on the final range of hills before the coastline. The venerable parsonage was dark and gloomy, enclosed by thick conifers and other woodland and hidden from any public view around a long, winding driveway.

The vicar had been incumbent since 1960, and this was now 1983. He originally had two churches, but one had recently been declared redundant and had been sold, now converted rather well into a private residence.

When I took up my diocesan post, he therefore had only one church in which to minister, and he was within a couple of years of retirement. He is probably the most detached shepherd of the flock that I came across in my career, clearly regarding his pastoral and liturgical duties as entirely superfluous to his personal interests.

He had a very fine model railway laid out upstairs in the house, to which he devoted most of his energies and attention. He also had a black-and-white television set and was a devotee of the new TV series such as *The Forsyte Saga*.

If his model train timetable or favourite television programme conflicted with the advertised service times at his church, he simply failed to turn up and his dwindling congregation just shrugged their shoulders and went back home.

*

Also on the island ministered another good colleague of mine, a scion of one of the oldest established firms of agricultural land agents in the south of England and therefore a man after my own heart. He and his wife lived in possibly my favourite parsonage of all, a stone-built, stone-roofed house of the late nineteenth century and early twentieth, plain and uncluttered, H in shape and set in a very large, gently sloping garden down to a valley, along which ran a vintage steam railway. The canon was very far from being eccentric, but he did hold an unusual post from the bishop. As well as being parish priest, he was also the diocesan exorcism chaplain, called upon to deal with poltergeists and such other strange spirits that go bump in the night.

Anyone more down to earth, level-headed and cautious it would be hard to find. A true gentleman cleric of the old school.

THE PARSONS. SURELY A BREED APART?

*

Back inland in the same county stood a solid four-square parsonage of indeterminate period, set at low level below a busy main road that was forever casting stormwater down the driveway into a huge lake outside the front door, requiring visiting parishioners to remember to wear wellington boots. No number of French drains or complaints to the highways authority ever seemed to diminish the aquatic character of this property.

The vicar had been an agricultural engineer before ordination and could turn his hand to anything – after his own fashion. An obliging chap, he regularly told us in the office that we need not worry about repairs and maintenance to his house, as he would enjoy dealing with them himself.

In those days we only carried out electrical test and inspection reports on parsonages every ten years. (Nowadays the interval is five years.) One of these happened to coincide with the vicar's retirement, a circumstance which was just as well.

Our NICEIC electrical engineer had only been in the premises for about half an hour when he emerged white-faced and trembling. He dug out from the recesses of his van a folder containing a quantity of self-adhesive labels printed in bright red and yellow capital letters and proceeded to stick one to the front door and several others in prominent places. He then unplugged and pocketed the main board fuse and drove off in a hurry.

The little notices read: *SAFETY WARNING! This source of electricity has been disconnected.*

Unhappily, that was not the only difficulty. When the cleaning ladies from the parish went in a little later to wash and scrub in anticipation of a new arrival (never to appear, sadly, as the parish was absorbed into the benefice next door), they found no water from the taps. We discovered after much digging and enquiry that the rising main had rusted away some time previously and that the house had been reconnected to the water supply serving the adjacent farmyard. Presumably, the farmer had become puzzled over the meter reading and had informed the Water Board, which had simply severed and capped off the T-junction that at some point in the previous decade the vicar had regarded as the obvious solution to his problem.

*

Here is another, rather extreme, example of a clergyman defending his 'parson's freehold'. This freehold, incidentally, was in two parts. Firstly, he was entitled to the 'freehold of the living', namely his right to remain in that post for as long as he wished, and more or less doing whatever he chose to do. There was an ultimate bishop's sanction to defrock him and 'suspend the living', but things would have had to degenerate to an exceptional degree for that drastic step to be taken. I never knew a bishop prepared to go to such lengths. Bishops tend to be wise enough to devote their pastoral skills to encouraging the miscreant concerned to resign instead.

The secondary right, following on from the first, was the freehold of the parsonage house. (His further titular personal rights to the other property of the benefice – the parish church(es) – and to the glebe were constrained by ecclesiastical law far too tortuous to go into here.)

Of course, by the 1970s and '80s, he could no longer sell, demolish, replace or abandon his parsonage purely according to his private whim. By then, General Synod of the Church of England had laid down rules (principally in 1938 and 1947) introducing an impressive system of mandatory consultation with diocese, patron, parochial church council and Church Commissioners introducing hoops that were difficult to jump through unilaterally.

Nonetheless, if the incumbent of the benefice, the parson, disagreed with any proposal to do any of those things, that was the end of the matter. His signature was required on the conveyance.

(Parsons could let their property, or parts of it, on an annual basis, but any such letting automatically ceased on the date of the parson's resignation or retirement. The tenant had no right to continue in occupation beyond that date, a provision which overrode any secular Rent Act protection. For this reason, a parson was incapable in law of granting a lease. Ecclesiastical Measures have the equivalence of Acts of Parliament, one of the advantages of the Established Church.)

Well, on then to an old market town, a quiet, sleepy place prone in those days to serious floods from the major river nearby (and, regrettably, prone in recent years to being a notorious regional venue for drug dealing). The rectory was a huge eighteenth-/early nineteenth-century edifice with a very fine south-facing garden aspect and rather complex

Fig. 6

rambling parts of an earlier age at its rear. The house stood right in the centre of the town, its rather disappointing main entrance door being stuck on the narrow end that had a brief frontage onto the public pavement (*Fig. 6*). The entire remainder of the demesne was hidden behind a high boundary wall, offering total seclusion.

The incumbent, another canon, was a cleric in true traditional mould. I gathered that a little before my time he had become increasingly irritated by suggestions and proposals from the diocese that the rectory should be replaced with something a little less expensive to maintain, of which there was in fact plenty of good choice around the town.

By the time I took up my post and entered his firing line, he had clearly had enough. He resolutely declined to respond to any diocesan communication of any kind, and although I tried a few times to invite myself to come and have a chat, it was a year or two before I was permitted beyond the doorstep. Eventually, when the subject of replacement had been dropped and he was near retirement, he did graciously let me in as far as the scullery, where we had a polite conversation about nothing in particular.

The highlight of this story, however, is that he had taken extreme umbrage against the archdeaconry surveyor we then engaged on parsonage building works in those days (before we employed an in-house diocesan surveyor in 1990 who began to transform the technical side of property management across the whole diocese, with impressive success, developing a highly profitable service to other Church-related organisations at commercial fees).

We used to use four architects in private practice, one for each archdeaconry, to manage parsonage maintenance and design the new houses we built in large numbers in the 1980s. This particular architect/surveyor had evidently been pushing the canon too hard over the replacement issue.

One day, the surveyor called at the rectory to carry out a regular quinquennial inspection for the normal diocesan maintenance routine and was met at the door by the rector brandishing his shotgun. My colleague did not stay to enquire whether it was loaded but beat a hasty retreat and never again went near the place.

A rather awkward provision of the Repair of Benefice Buildings Measure 1972 was that not only was a parsonage survey to be carried out every five years but that it was our legal obligation to complete the recommended repairs within twelve months of the date of the report. A nice question of law arose then in this case, as to whether any obligation subsisted where there was no prospect whatsoever of such a date arising in the foreseeable future.

*

Ecclesiastical law has its own eccentricities too, sometimes weeded out in subsequent amending legislation in light of unfortunate unforeseen consequences, sometimes not.

A good example was a feature of the original Pastoral Measure 1968, which covered somewhat peripherally the process for disposing of a parsonage house rendered redundant through the reorganisation of a benefice or its parishes.

With its roots in the far distant days when parsonages and church buildings were largely sited and built at the personal expense of landed private patrons (those persons entitled to present clergy to the 'living' of which they were patron), the Measure granted the patron first refusal on the purchase of the redundant house, at agreed valuation and without the property being exposed to the market.

In one village, an extremely posh and unreasonably pretty group of houses on the very eastern edge of the diocese, lay the perfect classical Georgian rectory in all its soft, old, glowing brick beauty, hidden from the road by ancient leafage and looking out over a glorious lawn at the rear to the unspoiled countryside beyond. Tragically, it came up for the chop as a parsonage, and the Pastoral Measure swung into play.

The patron, a knight of the realm, whose family certainly had not provided the house originally, chose to exercise his patronal right. This narked the archdeacon and me, as we were expecting to make an absolute bomb in sky-high bidding at public auction. Between the parties we agreed the name of a local valuation surveyor, who put a cautious conservative figure on the property from a selection of recent 'comparables' in the area, of which in reality there were precious few.

The deal was done, but the golden egg was not quite what Sir X had originally anticipated. It transpired that about twenty-five years previously, the then rector had casually permitted parishioners to take a shortcut to church along the gravel terrace that ran the full length of the garden frontage of the house, feet from the dignified sash windows of all the principal rooms. This informal arrangement had continued uninterrupted ever since.

Now, redundancy of a venerable parsonage might sometimes have had the grudging acceptance of the parochial church council and much of the congregation but very often the total antipathy of many village residents who never darkened the doors of the church. (This was frequently even more violent in the case of redundancy of the church building as a place of worship, when I would be able to guarantee physical opposition from villagers who had not been inside the building since their own infant baptism.)

In this case, a local resident decided to have a chat with the rights of way officer at the district council. Following advice received, he circulated the community with a survey for names and signatures and affirmations of the length of time and frequency with which the gravel terrace had been used by all and sundry, submitting it shortly afterwards to the council offices.

I did my best, but it was a hopeless case. Beyond the shadow of a doubt the route qualified for adoption as a registered public footpath, as over the decades and changes in freeholder, no 'let or hindrance' had ever been applied. A public right of way was duly designated, and the value of the former rectory promptly plummeted.

*

The next piece of Church history does truly beggar belief, but again I must claim the accuracy of my record. Readers of a sensitive disposition might prefer to skip this anecdote, as it is really rather unsavoury.

This rectory was an attractive, modest building that had been the Victorian village school, to which had been added a sympathetic tile-hung upper storey and a pitched roof to make into a parsonage sometime, I believe, in the early 1960s.

The rector lived there with his wife and an adult daughter who, in modern parlance, had 'learning difficulties' and occupied a little bedsit of her own upstairs.

The suffragan bishop, an excellent colleague of mine as Chairman of the Parsonages Committee, began to receive reports from the rural dean that communicant churchgoers in the parish were going down with mysterious food poisoning on an alarming scale. The rural dean had made tactful enquiries and had discovered that the communion wafers were homemade little biscuits or breads from the kitchen of the rectory. The rector's wife had been a good cook in her time, but she and her husband were now well into their eighties and perhaps she was losing her touch.

Bishop John and I debated how best to investigate, and we hatched a plan to invite ourselves to the rectory for afternoon tea. At appropriate intervals we would each in turn excuse ourselves from the drawing room, ostensibly to visit the lavatory but, if possible, to sneak a quick look around other parts of the ground floor, to form some idea of how this aged couple were managing. I think the bishop had in mind the opportunity to suggest to the parson that he really ought to consider retirement.

Well, we both turned up one day and were graciously invited to take tea. We declined the offer of biscuits. Bishop John was the first to try his luck, but unfortunately the rector accompanied him from the room in order to show his lordship where the facilities were located and hovered in the hall in order to escort him back. Possibly by that point the parson had begun to smell a rat about the true motive for this episcopal visitation and was beginning to feel nervous.

My chance came twenty minutes later, and Bishop John stymied any attempt by the parson to keep me in sight by explaining exactly where I would find the downstairs cloakroom.

I made a beeline for the kitchen quarters.

It is at this point that fragile readers may wish to look away.

Along the hallway, on which every surface was layered in grey dust, was the closed kitchen door. This I opened cautiously so as not to make a sound. Immediately beyond was the open door into the scullery, or utility room. Staring at me there was a large goat. Framed in the doorway, it was standing, or rather squelching, in nine inches of compacted, oozing straw covering the entire floor of the scullery. A trickle of brown liquid ran across the kitchen floor, to which I then turned my horrified attention.

Piled in tottering heaps on the floor were towers of unwashed plain white crockery to which were adhered the greasy remains of dinners and teas from what (judging by the mould growth) must have included the distant past. The colour of the linoleum was indiscernible.

Unlike the rector, who had merely 'smelled a rat', I could see two, sniffing at me from opposite corners of the room. Clear, straight rat runs criss-crossed the remaining space between plates, cups, saucers and kitchen furniture.

The enamel sink and drainer were laden with open bags of wood chippings and sheep nuts, presumably for the benefit of the goat.

I quietly retreated, closing the door behind me and tiptoeing down to the lavatory at the far end of the hall, where I pulled the flushing chain and returned to the tea party. I looked meaningfully at the bishop, declining a top-up from the teapot and shortly afterwards we made our excuses and returned to the car.

This was, of course, long before the era of mobile phones with inbuilt cameras, but I kicked myself for not having brought with me my pocket-sized Kodak Instamatic. The photographic record would have been part of social history. But later on, I thought, well, what purpose would a photo have really served, except to emphasise, or even publicise, the mental and physical frailties of an elderly couple who had devoted their lives to the pastoral interests of their parishioners?

It was only a few months later that the rector died suddenly in his sleep. His widow closely followed him.

Our wise and excellent glebe agent, himself an ordained minister as well as chartered surveyor and local farmer, soon found some alternative accommodation for the bereaved daughter near his own farm.

The first specialist firm of industrial cleaners of contaminated premises that I engaged called at the empty rectory but declined to give me a quotation. The second charged an arm and a leg but made a good job of it.

I never established what happened to the goat.

*

Until well into the 1990s, many parish priests in the Church of England had been lifelong bachelors. I don't know the reason for this, but perhaps it was still a residual echo of the old monastic tradition. Celibacy in the Roman Catholic Church is based upon the concept of being married to the Church, but this was unlikely to be the motive for the single priests that I knew, many of whom were 'low church' Protestants.

Having no family commitments, they were usually supremely diligent and effective parish parsons, always out and about visiting and organising activities for young and old alike. They knew everybody, and everyone knew them. Some were exceptional, staying up all night at the bedside of a dying parishioner or running errands for the housebound.

Most were, in my experience, truly monastic in their own personal lifestyle, scarcely feeding themselves adequately and living in self-imposed simplicity and discomfort. Their mind and intellect were on other things: the holiday club for the children; the liturgy; specialist interests in flora, fauna, literature, theology or language; just being there for people.

One example of monastic life in a parsonage was the incumbent in one vicarage, a mid-nineteenth-century brick mansion of a place with five or six bedrooms and attics to boot. He lived there all alone for most of his ministry and possessed a wealth of very fine antique furniture inherited from his ancient family, which he cared for meticulously. Large as it was, the parsonage only just managed to house this vast collection. Well into old age, he consistently refused to retire, because no home in retirement could possibly have accommodated all his furniture.

In common with many parsons of his generation, he never bothered with heating the house. By the late 1970s, we had installed conventional central heating into virtually all our parsonages, usually during vacancies (known as interregna). When a bachelor was appointed, we knew we were in for trouble, because he would never turn on the oil-fired boiler, and this would quietly rust away in disuse.

My ally Bishop John N used to tell me that whenever he went to stay overnight with any of his clergy, which in those days was a normal routine for episcopal visitations, he would always take with him a large black plastic bin liner or groundsheet. If the visit was to one of these monastic colleagues, the plastic liner would invariably be needed, to put beneath the bed sheet to keep out the damp.

*

Not all our clergy enjoyed happy relations with their neighbours. In a large conurbation, I bought an excellent spacious house for a newly established assistant curacy post. The parish was largely a deprived community with great social needs, and the local church was doing good work and expanding in numbers.

The garden of this property was very narrow, the rear boundary fence running parallel to the lengthy house only about eight yards from its windows. The garden was back-to-back with the lawn of the bungalow in the adjoining street, occupied by a man and wife who never conversed with one another at less than full volume. They had two excessively unruly children who had inherited this trait. Their combined communicative content, moreover, was unremittingly foul, blasphemous and sexually odious.

The young curate and his family, after a while, simply could not take it any longer. His vicar appealed to us in the end to find another house somewhere else. This we did, and I always pitied our unwitting purchasers of the original house. Maybe they could give as good as they got.

*

PARSONAGE AND PARSON

Another example of disastrous neighbour relations took place in a suburban parish on the outskirts of a military town. The parsonage was one of a row of respectable 1950's villas, each with a large rear garden separated from its neighbour by a panel fence or hedge, the overall layout of the estate being four-square and consistent. Every boundary was a straight line, and all the corners were right angles.

For some reason which I never discovered, the adjacent householder to one side of the vicarage had taken umbrage with the parson over some deemed slight or other, connected I believe with wedding arrangements. At any rate, this neighbour seemed to have developed a hatred verging on paranoia and was determined to make the poor vicar's life as miserable as possible.

I entered the fray when the neighbour, unknown to the vicar, wrote to the diocesan bishop claiming that this dreadful parson had rearranged the boundary fence at the dead of night and incorporated part of the neighbour's shrub border into his own garden. In consequence he, the neighbour, had felt obliged to install CCTV on a tall pole, pointing directly into the vicarage garden. He further claimed that the infra-red CCTV footage had revealed the vicar on his hands and knees in the dark, grubbing out the evidence of the illegal tampering with the line of the fence.

The bishop passed this missive on to me without comment and rather rashly instructed the vicar to explain himself, as this sort of thing did the reputation of the Church no good at all.

I went to see the situation for myself. The vicar was beside himself with anger when I showed him the letter and took me out to inspect the garden boundary and also the camera on the pole, which had a clear view not only of the garden but of the vicar's study window.

The boundary line seemed to me to be as straight as a die, and I saw no evidence of disturbance to any of the fence posts or panels. I took some measurements and returned to the office to find the original conveyance plan.

I was quickly satisfied that the accusation was wholly unjustified and informed the bishop and vicar accordingly. They asked me to write firmly to the neighbour in appropriate terms.

There followed a somewhat acrimonious correspondence, and sadly the vicar's woes were not at an end. With the reluctant consent of the bishop, he moved out to live in a house the far side of town that he had acquired for his retirement and commuted back to his parish each day.

We let the vicarage, and the tenants apparently found the neighbour most friendly and quite delightful.

*

My next case (this is beginning to sound like a psychiatrist's report) also involves a parson who, in a much more amusing and teasing sense, scarcely inhabited his vicarage.

His parsonage was the oldest we had, dating from the very early 1600s, although it had only been Church property in the modern era. It was truly enormous, with a fine, level garden boasting a magnificent old blue cedar.

He, the canon, was another of these clerical bachelors. I knew him well because he also worked part-time in the

Diocesan Office as Communications Officer and Editor of the diocesan magazine. He was great fun, with a refreshing sense of humour and a laid-back attitude to Church rigmarole. He drew the brilliant cartoons that graced the covers of the series of informative and advisory leaflets that I produced on every conceivable subject for the benefit and education of ordained occupants of parsonages. These ranged from the deleterious effects of Superser portable liquid gas heaters, through to basic maintenance tips like changing tap washers and clearing gutters, on to strict guidance on the prevention of unauthorised rights of way and an explanation of benefaction grants for undertaking small improvements (not involving Kango hammers). Several other subjects were added. I decided on cartoon covers because I thought the contents would be more likely to be read. Latterly, towards the end of my time, the humourless hierarchy insisted on plain corporate covers in tasteful print with the dreadful new Church of England 'logo'. I bet the leaflets were never read from that time onwards.

Anyway, back to the canon. Here was a parish priest who really was immersed in his local community. He did not merely have his own personal tankard in the Green Dragon across the road as, often as not, he was the chap pulling the pints behind the bar. Truly a man at home among friends.

*

Some clergy left their parsonage to engage in the local community. Others brought the community services right inside the house. One such vicar's vicarage had a lovely classical and symmetrical frontage in warm cream stone. A huge timber-frame barn, blackened in bitumen, stood alongside, almost as old as the house. The roadside appearance was only marred by the newly rebuilt low-boundary wall constructed unforgivably (and before my time, I hasten to add) in shiny yellow brick.

The vicar was also one of our four archdeacons. At that time, all our archdeacons also had the care of a small parish each, just to keep their feet firmly on the ground. Not long before, indeed, the archdeacon of our central district had the large, bustling urban parish in the middle of our cathedral city and the busy civic church that went with it. He was still able to fulfil his archidiaconal duties. (He went on to become a senior diocesan bishop himself.) In my view, it was a mistake to appoint subsequent archdeacons without a parochial post. This turned them into executive officers and rather disconnected administrators. One or two overcame this obstacle. One or two did not.

Our committee structure for policy on clergy housing I inherited from my predecessor and found it to be very sound. We had a small committee for each archdeaconry, comprising a mix of clergy, clergy wives and laity from the local area concerned. We made frequent site visits together to the various houses to consider issues that arose, and so every member was very familiar with the buildings within their remit. A single diocesan committee, such as is common in other dioceses, would never have had that fundamentally important benefit. Each of the four committees met every two months, and for most of my tenure, these meetings were held in the home of the archdeacon concerned. (One of my earliest archdeacons and his wife always gave me a slap-up lunch afterwards.)

At the vicarage, we would meet in the drawing room around a coffee table usually laden with cups, pots and biscuits. Very often at the same time in the dining room, the local doctor's surgery would be in full swing, patients waiting on upright chairs in the hallway. The comings and goings of patients, nurses and clergy housing committee members could sometimes cause a degree of organisational misunderstanding in that vicarage – even occasionally some surprising revelations.

This archdeacon was also one of the volunteer drivers of the community bus which took people shopping and visiting in the absence of a regular bus service in that very rural area. A good man (and a fine cook).

*

In the far north-east corner of the diocese was a large, scrubby area of unkempt land on which stood the dilapidated remains of an old brick outbuilding that had once formed part of a rectory demesne. The house and garden had long since been sold away, decades before my time, but I remained responsible for this odd residual ground that for some reason (soon to be discovered) had deliberately been omitted from the sale.

Such pieces of land, retained for whatever purpose from the disposal of parsonage house and grounds, assumed a rather curious legal title. They became what was unsurprisingly called 'parsonage land'. This title could not be disposed of without the express consent of the Church Commissioners in London, unlike diocesan glebe which was within the discretion of the diocese.

The difficulty in this case was that it might very well have been glebe. There was no way of knowing. Ancient glebe originated from Tudor times, and title deeds were non-existent. Sales of glebe therefore had to be defined by means of a 'statutory declaration' in each case. These would be made before a local solicitor who was a 'commissioner for oaths' either by the glebe agents or by me. We simply had to be satisfied, by diocesan records prior to 1978 and rent receipts since, that the land was ours.

Some clergy, who were newly in post in 1978, were rather vague as to the identity or location of the glebe they had inherited from their predecessors. It was all largely word of mouth or rather scrappy paperwork. I have always been convinced that this personal glebe management and record-keeping by parsons, prior to the adoption of professional management, has lost many acres of ground quietly into the deemed ownership of adjoining landowners, notably the great estates that acquired the old monastic and abbey grounds from Henry VIII following the dissolution of monasteries.

Back to this patch of land. I decided that a close personal inspection was needed, and so one day I drove up there to poke around. I found evidence that the half-ruined building had, until very recently, been occupied. Old bits of furniture and furnishings still lay about, and some rusting children's toys were still out on the grass. I happened then to meet an elderly dog walker, who providentially remembered what had occurred. The last parson at the rectory had taken pity on a young, homeless couple thirty years previously and had let them live in the outbuilding on the understanding that they would have to make it basically habitable at their own expense.

The young family was still there when the rector came to sell the property, and so he arranged simply that the area and building used by these young folk should be excluded from the sale.

They were still there, now in late middle age, only until a few months before my visit in 1981.

The property was a hazardous structure, and I needed to sell. Was it 'parsonage land' or glebe? I had to go to London to find out.

*

The early 1980s were probably the peak of the fortunes, status and reputation of that august body, the Church Commissioners for England. They occupied the entire premises of the stately edifice on the north bank of the Thames, No. 1 Millbank, London. They employed doormen, porters and sundry flunkies in dark blue uniform and peaked cap. The floors and wood panelling everywhere were spotless and polished, the huge gilt-framed oil portraits of former archbishops, first estate commissioners, second estate commissioners and third (respectively archbishops of Canterbury, members of the House of Commons and the persons who actually chaired the committees) gazed down from on high. When I first visited them, by formal invitation, even the Secretary (the executive boss) was an Honourable.

Before the big property crash of 1988/89, their financial star was in the ascendant, and they could do no wrong. They had two main functions: to manage their eye-watering investment portfolio, which they were at the time gradually readjusting away from a heavy historical dependence on agricultural land and into the financial markets; and to act as charity regulator for all parsonages, glebe and closed places of worship throughout the country.

The latter role today is much lighter in touch than then, decision-taking having been largely devolved to dioceses. Back then, their officers severely micromanaged by way of strict consent procedures. Every design for a new parsonage, for instance, had to be vetted by their own architects' department, and long were the arguments to and fro about the size of the bathroom or the use of stone instead of brick. Their word was law because they provided much of the money.

On the investment front, I will share with you a serious rumour which was circulating at the time. Apparently, their senior investments manager, inspecting their real estate assets in the USA from time to time, transported himself there and back by booked passage on the liner the *Queen Elizabeth*, having sent aboard in advance a suitable quantity of his preferred vintage wines. Perhaps it was just a rumour. Perhaps it was not all on expenses.

Pride, however, cometh before a fall. Investment returns needed, quite rightly, to be diverted away from parsonage grants and annual subsidies to dioceses, towards a fully funded pension pot for the accelerating number of retiring clergy, principally those who had been caught up in the wave of ordinations at the end of World War II.

Certain development land purchases, prior to any planning permission, received a bad press (not entirely justified in hindsight).

Money was becoming tight, and this great institutional monolith was becoming an unaffordable dinosaur.

Latterly, towards the end of my time, the doors were finally closed on No. 1 Millbank, and the staffing drastically reduced. Today, this modest institution occupies a single open-plan floor of Church House Westminster, sharing the facilities with a variety of other Anglican bodies. How are the mighty fallen.

(The patch of ground proved in the end to be deemed glebe, simply by virtue of the elapse in time since the sale of the benefice parsonage house.)

Despite the trials and tribulations of the Commissioners as an organisation over this period, I must record my unfailing appreciation of every one of their officers with whom I had any dealings during my thirty-one years. Without exception, they were well informed, helpful and courteous, many with a welcome sense of humour.

FOUR

WHAT ELSE CAN WE USEFULLY DO WITH THESE PROPERTIES?

A few of our older parsonages had extensive grounds, originally comprising a pleasure garden, kitchen garden and park. These were the maintenance responsibility of the parson living there, a costly and time-consuming burden in many cases. Sometimes his parochial church council offered to help pay for grass cutting, but the local church had no duty whatsoever so far as the parsonage was concerned.

By far the largest was the park, dotted with splendid mature hardwoods, surrounding a former vicarage which had been retained for occupation by my Glebe Committee Chairman Bishop John N. This house had a feature in common with most of these large demesnes. It sat firmly in the centre of the grounds, thereby preventing a reduction in acreage by carving off a chunk to sell to a neighbour, or as a building plot.

PARSONAGE AND PARSON

A rare exception was the garden of the rectory in the centre of an old Hardy town. The long, wide garden had the house at one end on the street front, while a field gate at the opposite end gave onto a grassy space owned by the district council, adjoining a public road at the rear. The grounds had been part of a much larger acreage running with the early parsonage house which had been demolished in the 1950s.

The town suffered from poor employment prospects for its local young people and a severe shortage of houses and flats at reasonable rents.

I had set up an initiative a few years earlier for the grant of long ground leases of glebe on the outskirts of villages to some of the smaller housing associations serving the counties of the diocese, to build on each patch half a dozen affordable houses. The lease terms strictly confined occupancy, including all subsequent occupiers, to those with an established local connection, either by family or employment. Priority was to those in the civil parish concerned, and if at any time there were insufficient candidates, then they were drawn from adjacent parishes determined by a geographical series of concentric circles. Almost none of these glebe sites would have been granted planning permission for conventional sale but were approved for affordable local housing. They were not 'social housing' for those on state benefits or dispossessed from council houses; they were for folk with jobs or family commitments that limited their income to a level that put market rents out of reach.

I would always hold a public meeting, arranged with the civil parish council and usually the housing association, to explain well in advance what we were hoping to achieve. 'Nimbyism' was often rife, and some of those meetings were decidedly sticky. I came away battered and bruised (metaphorically speaking) on several such occasions. Regrettably, some of the loudest antagonistic voices were those of Church members.

However, we ploughed on, and in most cases by the time the houses (always vernacular in style) were completed and occupied, the neighbours soon found that they knew most of the residents' families and proved to be perfectly friendly.

All in all, we leased six sites across three counties producing fifty-two affordable homes in perpetuity (well, ninety-nine to 125 years anyway). The flagship site of twenty homes, with their thatched roofs and flint walls, proved to be a planning blueprint for the famous new town of Poundbury in Dorset, promoted by the Prince of Wales, which began construction a year or so later.

You think I am exaggerating? Well, Prince Charles himself opened our little glebe scheme there (*Fig. 7*) and cut the ribbon, flying in by helicopter specially for the purpose.

My determination to involve the Church in a practical contribution to alleviate the rapidly growing problem of unaffordable housing in its rural areas led me to a wider interest in the subject, and in 1996 I became a trustee of the Churches National Housing Coalition, and then a founder trustee of its successor 'Housing Justice', the only overtly Christian charity in England and Wales promoting the cause of the homeless and poorly housed. I retired from this in 2018 but remained involved in their Welsh initiatives.

Fig. 7

I have digressed. Back to the garden. The rector was a very socially minded parson and was enthusiastic when I tentatively suggested trying something similar to these glebe schemes, on the lower half of his garden. We found a local charitable housing association, which wanted to take a very innovative approach. The first hurdle was to obtain rights of access from our rear field gate across the council land to the road. The council could have been mercenary if they chose, demanding money for releasing their 'ransom strip'. Fortunately, when they heard what we had in mind, they granted a vehicular right of way without charge.

The next step was to transfer the area from parsonage to glebe, so that it could be leased. A parson, if you remember, cannot grant lettings beyond his own term of appointment.

WHAT ELSE CAN WE USEFULLY DO WITH THESE PROPERTIES?

The ground lease to the housing association was completed and a building contractor appointed to construct two low blocks of apartments comprising four flats each. The eventual lettings were to be designated for eight young persons aged eighteen to twenty-four who could demonstrate that they were local, unemployed and potentially homeless.

Eight were chosen by careful interview, who had to show particular commitment to their side of the bargain.

They would each have to be involved physically in the construction of their flats, under supervision by a 'training master' who was an experienced working foreman with the building contractors.

They would also have to attend, initially full-time, at the nearby technical college to acquire a vocational qualification in the trade of their choice.

The additional cost of the training and supervision was met by a grant from the EU Social Fund and the district council.

All eight completed their responsibilities and moved into their flats.

We had provided a home, a skill and a qualification for each of those young people. All bar one obtained local employment in the building trades, and several have done very well.

FIVE
GENEROSITY OR CHAOS?

In the old days, a great many parish clergy in parsonages with large gardens quite naturally chose to make land available for use by the local community, rather than pay a gardener to cut acres of grass just to maintain the parson's privacy.

They would erect, often at their own private expense, youth huts, parish halls and even public lavatories, at the far end of their parsonage grounds, without giving a thought to future implications for occupancy rights, establishment of possessory title or separate secular use.

Over the subsequent decades (and in some cases centuries), the ownership of such areas of parsonage grounds became decidedly vague, especially in those cases where documentary title for the original parsonage domain was unclear or altogether absent.

Sooner or later, argument would ensue, hackles would be raised, solicitors' letters would fly around like confetti; harsh words would be exchanged with neighbours or with the civil parish council, or disputes would arise over maintenance responsibilities.

All these would have to be resolved, and it was one of my duties to enter the fray and bring these issues as best I could to a satisfactory conclusion.

A cursory reference to the index of parishes in the current Diocesan Handbook immediately brings to mind at least fifteen such battles in which I was engaged in those thirty years of management. All had pastoral implications as well as practical or legal ones, and liaison with the relevant archdeacon was vital.

In the 1980s, archdeacons were figures of unquestioned authority and presence.[2]

Parish clergy defied them at their peril. I was witness to a classic example of an archdeacon's physical influence one day outside a rectory. I forget the cause of the archidiaconal wrath on that occasion but vividly remember him chasing the rector around the perimeter of the house, kicking him severely in his substantial rump every few yards while wagging a finger and expressing his ire in colourful language for the entire circuit around the building.

*

---

[2] An uncle of my own, as Archdeacon of Suffolk, was surely the last of that ilk to wear frock coat, breeches and clerical buttoned gaiters for weddings and funerals.

PARSONAGE AND PARSON

Here follow some highlights from these cases of challenged ownership or responsibility arising from former acts of generosity by landed parsons.

In one tiny village, the modern vicarage stands in very extensive grounds that were originally part of the vast former parsonage on the other side of a private road. The site of the present house, along with the private road, a car park and a nineteenth-century parish hall, had been transferred out of parsonage ownership into glebe when the old house had been sold in the 1960s.

Or had they?

Documentary title relied on an eighteenth-century map of such rudimentary representation and cartographical inaccuracy that the features it purported to record were quite unrecognisable on the ground.

In recent years, the parish hall had ceased to be used for church activities and had been let (by the parochial church council, which probably had no jurisdiction) to a nursery school. As a result, the little car park was becoming overcrowded with the 4x4 Chelsea tractors that the young mums all considered essential to the transportation of their tiny offspring to and from the nursery. The road was becoming blocked, obstructing access not only to the hall but also to the vicarage and a public footpath running nearby.

Please would the vicar do something?

Well, the vicar of course phoned me up and appealed for help.

Who controlled the car park and the hall? The parochial church council.

Who enjoyed the substantial rental income from the nursery school? The parochial church council.

Who was actually entitled to receive that rent and lay down the law on the use of the car park? If they were glebe, then the Diocesan Board of Finance. But if they were still, in fact, parsonage property, then the income was payable to the incumbent vicar, who then must declare it as a fee and have it deducted from his stipend.

What a conundrum.

I can recall at least three very similar situations. All of them had an additional factor that had to be taken into account. One parish hall, an enormous timber youth hut and a purpose-built brick parish office were all in a severe state of dilapidation. Any claim of ownership would bring with it the inevitable obligation to accept responsibility for repair, renovation, safety improvements, legal compliance, replacement or demolition.

The largest such white elephant was a cavernous, green, corrugated-iron-clad parish hall in parsonage grounds, used daily by a variety of organisations as it stood in the centre of a market town.

In most such cases where legal title was found to be a diocesan responsibility but in practice a parish resource, I was quick to persuade all concerned that a prompt transfer of the freehold to the parochial church council, free of charge, was the best solution.

There were other situations, however, where we discovered old residues of parsonage property that now had much lucrative potential. The houses and gardens might well have been sold long ago, but, for good reason at the time, certain trackways or entrances were retained by the Church for purposes that had long since ceased to apply.

They became forgotten, neglected and unrecorded until, suddenly, their true title emerged into the light of day.

One such was the large entrance and visibility splay onto the public road from both a modern vicarage and an adjacent former vicarage. A new owner of the old house obtained planning permission to build three houses in the extensive grounds. As we still owned the entire shared entranceway, and although the former vicarage had a covenanted right of way, there was no right of access for any additional independent properties.

We made a lot of money from the grant of access rights in that case, as we did for a precisely similar scenario. Of course, we received a great deal of local flak as a result, the 'money-grubbing diocese' being a perpetually popular target of abuse in parishes, especially rural ones. Diplomatic skills were required in earnest.

In one parish, the 1960's vicarage stood in a large garden next to St Nicholas church. The church enjoyed a constant stream of visitors all year round, as it contained the most exquisite, engraved glass windows by Laurence Whistler, and Lawrence of Arabia was buried in the graveyard. The building had suffered severe bomb damage in October 1940, and in 1955 Sir Laurence began his series of thirteen engraved lights.

Sometime in the 1970s or early '80s, the vicar became fed up with visitors knocking on his door and asking to use the vicarage lavatory, so he persuaded his parochial church council to pay for the construction of a loo with washbasin

GENEROSITY OR CHAOS?

as an attachment to the side of the vicarage, where water and drainage was, of course, easy to connect.

This arrangement worked happily for many years, until the house became pastorally redundant, and I had to sell it.

Oh dear, what a fuss. As well as being up in arms over the loss of their parsonage house, the village was now faced with the confiscation of their very public lavatory, by now regularly used by the church congregation as well as tourists, visitors and walkers.

As representative of those dreadful pen-pushers at the diocese, I attended a local meeting to hear them out, accompanied by the archdeacon and rural dean. I was presented with a plan for a new, expanded lavatory building with separate facilities for men and women, to be located in one corner of the parsonage garden that had been the compost heap, up against the boundary of the churchyard.

It was architect designed and very splendid, with a long access ramp for disabled people running alongside the church steps but on the vicarage side of the boundary.

The implication was clear, and we went along with it. The area of land concerned was reserved out of the vicarage sale and passed without charge into the ownership of the PCC. I think we also made a monetary contribution acknowledging the cost incurred by the parish for the original lavatory space.

This case was the seed of a new fruitful policy we adopted for all subsequent parsonage sales. We would in future make a grant to the local Church, up to a certain standard limit, out of the sale proceeds, if the parish made a convincing case that the parsonage or its grounds had provided an

PARSONAGE AND PARSON

established tangible resource for parish purposes beyond being simply the residence of their parson.

Needless to say, we ended up making such a grant on virtually every occasion. Some of the claims were pretty nebulous, but it was a useful exercise in oiling the wheels of redundancy to keep the locals happy.

The extreme example of parochial triumph in this regard was the modern parsonage in the centre of our cathedral city. It was built on purchased land, only feet from the west door of its parish church, in the 1970s.

Under pressure from the rector, who had a vulnerable young family, we agreed to buy a house out in the suburbs as a new rectory, because at that time the city centre after dark was a rowdy and often violent area, replete as it was with several bars and pubs.

However, by then the city-centre rectory had been largely taken over by the parish as a space for meeting rooms, parish secretary's office and a coffee retreat for parishioners. The parsonage accommodation had gradually retreated upstairs and was now confined to the second floor.

It goes without saying that none of this parochial invasion of the parsonage had ever received the consent of the Diocesan Parsonages Committee, as it had never been sought.

When we agreed to evacuate the family to a more tranquil part of the city, we informed the parish that they would have to 'up sticks' and let us sell the vacated property. That concentrated minds, and the very competent vice chairman of the PCC was deputed to negotiate with me, which led to a happy acquaintance of mutual respect.

GENEROSITY OR CHAOS?

The PCC decided that the best solution was to buy the property themselves and discount the purchase price as much as they could by the diocesan 'Loss of Amenity' grant which at that time was a standard ten per cent of the sale price.

One way and another, they succeeded in acquiring a fine city-centre property with private garage and parking space for a most reasonable sum. I seem to remember that even this sum was paid over to us in several well-spaced instalments.

*

One or two of our houses, in contrast, were never going to interest their parish – nor indeed anyone else except the clergyman and his family who lived there.

Clergy became very attached to their home, particularly those who had been incumbent of their benefice for more than a quarter of a century – not an unusual tenure in those days.

One couple, a rector and his wife, had raised a family in their parsonage and were now on their own but were wholly devoted to the house.

Unfortunately, it was very slowly sinking into the ground. The water table on the site of the house and garden was only about four inches below ground level in normal weather conditions and about two inches above the ground in wet weather. The foundations were gradually getting lower and lower, unfortunately not at an even rate. In consequence, the internal door frames, on both floors, were now parallelograms rather than rectangles, and none of the solid 1920's doors could close. The plaster on the ceilings and interior brick walls was cracked and crazed but, being bound in good old horsehair, remained in place.

We tried to drain the water away from the house foundations by digging a deep moat around the outside walls and filling it with washed shingle. Rather optimistically, we laid land drains away from the moat in all directions, but they tended to work in reverse and swamp the moat with groundwater from elsewhere in the garden. Pedestrian access to the house needed gumboots in all seasons, and over the years the front hall, reached up several steps to the front door, became merely a depository for muddy footwear. No matter, the rector was a true countryman and these things never fazed him.

SIX
WHAT – YOU MEAN THERE'S MORE?

At this point it is necessary to veer away from the focus on parsonage houses, in order to record some of my experiences with two other forms of ecclesiastical property, but which equally enjoyed the eccentricity and/or delight mooted in the title of this book.

Firstly, a project which I tried to promote on some of our agricultural glebe, of which we had in those days about two thousand acres.

Most of the glebe was let in small acreages to local farmers. We had very few 'economic holdings', only two in excess of a hundred acres each, with just a handful of farm buildings. Only one holding had a farmhouse.

In many cases, the glebe in or near a village contained peripheral land such as scrub, rough woodland or wide road verges that was unproductive and not let.

The diocese took 'social responsibility' seriously and employed two full-time officers to promote it. One of them developed a strong pastoral concern for Gypsies and Travellers. At the time, our southernmost county was still a regular seasonal destination for traditional Romany gypsies, while further north nearer the motorway, 'New Age' and Irish Travellers frequently gathered. Ours was the first diocese in England to provide an ordained chaplain to Gypsies and Travellers, a role which dear Roger fulfilled with dedication, empathy and enthusiasm, setting a template for similar appointments elsewhere in the country.

In neither county was there adequate provision of sites for temporary stopping places or longer term serviced trailer parks. Consequently, Travellers parked wherever they could, committing trespass and causing antagonism with settled communities. Surely the solution that would relieve residents and Gypsies alike would be to set up modest stopping sites in secluded rural locations well away from village homes?

Surely the Church should set an example for other landowners to follow? Our Social Responsibility Officer, Kathleen, and I determined that this should be the case. I identified about half a dozen suitable places, and we agreed that as a priority, any such provision should include basic management such as foul waste disposal, rubbish collection and mains water. All were readily achievable at little expense.

Two glebe sites were found that had potential as permanent trailer parks, and a local housing association expressed interest in taking these on as 'flagship' pioneers for clean, tidy, landscaped pitches, providing a safe and secure environment for Traveller families with children, drug-free and hygienic. The housing association would manage them to the same standard as their dwellings, with a site manager present on weekdays.

The initiative led to regular meetings in our board room with representatives from county councils, education authorities, the police and the Traveller community to promote a wider role for the Church in Traveller welfare. I even contributed an article in the pivotal 1999 report *Gaining Ground: Law Reform for Gypsies & Travellers* produced by Cardiff Law School, which informed a debate in the House of Lords led by Lord Avebury.

My Parsonages & Glebe Committee went along with the glebe proposals, with the sole stipulation that in each case we must first hold a local consultative meeting with the parochial church council and invited civil councillors so that the matter was fully discussed before any decision was taken.

Well, of course, in retrospect now it is obvious that such an initiative would never get off the ground. The nuisance, confrontation, heavy-handed policing and sheer nastiness on both sides that were a well-publicised consequence of unauthorised Traveller sites in the 1990s all doomed our glebe scheme to abject failure.

The litmus tests were, inevitably, the local consultative meetings. I arranged these and attended with Kathleen, and we put the case each time as reasonably as we could. One or two PCCs heard us out and offered a measured response. Others were less courteous. One evening meeting in particular I recall, in a little village. In that parish, we had a small, secluded woodland separated from the village by a major modern bypass road that had severed all access connection between houses and glebe.

I have rarely experienced members of the Christian Church expressing themselves (the embarrassed rector excepted) in such colourfully violent language as at that appalling gathering. The raised voices were in fact a minority, the other local representatives choosing to remain silent.

As I crept out afterwards into the dark night to limp home with my tail between my legs, I was met by one of the locals who had said nothing during the meeting. "Thank you for coming," she whispered to me. "I am so glad that someone understands. My son went off to be a Traveller, and my husband and I have been ostracised here ever since."

*

I turn now to redundant churches or, more accurately in recent legislation, 'churches closed for public worship'. The new phrasing is certainly more apposite, as the buildings themselves rarely became redundant. They just took on a new life and purpose (*Fig. 8*), but not before a great deal of angst had been expended and tortuous bureaucratic process accomplished, often in the teeth of raw emotion and, in at least one case, physical violence.

By the time I retired in 2011, ninety-eight churches in the diocese had been declared redundant and withdrawn from use as regular places of worship. Of these, I dealt with

Fig. 8

thirty, all for an astonishing range of new uses and new owners, many of whom exceeded in eccentricity any of the parsons who had lately exercised their ministry beneath the leaky roofs of the buildings thrust into my temporary care.

One of my most entertaining cases was the former Church of St Osmund, in the centre of the diocese's largest conurbation. Early twentieth century, it was designed in high Romanesque fashion with a huge, hipped dome in copper toned to green. The rest of the roof was constructed of lightweight clinker concrete, but the corrosive nature of the clinker element had started to erode the steel reinforcement in the mix, with the result that bits of the ceiling underside of the roof began to fall onto the congregation and furnishings below. This was from a very great height, as the volume of the building was cathedral in its proportions.

PARSONAGE AND PARSON

The congregation escaped unscathed to worship in the adjacent hall annex, and in due course the future of this monumental town landmark was 'over to you, chum' and landed in my lap.

I had early hope of a prompt solution, as a famous symphony orchestra expressed an interest, as a rehearsal and training centre.

Their surveyor advised against.

In the meantime, I had to secure the building and deal with any urgent practical matters. Some of the decorative features were exquisite, not least the Eric Gill wall panels. The highlight for me, however – as an organist – was the incredible 1930's Compton pipe organ enclosed in an enormous swell box, in the same way as the great cinema organs of that era, and with a detached 'horseshoe' three-manual console. It was an historic masterpiece, listed Grade I by the British Institute of Organ Studies. One of my fondest memories is playing that instrument for half an hour at every one of my regular patrols of the building, letting rip to an otherwise empty and abandoned church interior that enjoyed an ambience much like the film set to *Ben Hur* or *Antony and Cleopatra*.

A less pleasant memory is fixing warning labels and padlocks to the organ blower room and boiler house deep underground beneath the nave, which were full of decomposing blue asbestos fibre insulating materials wafting like dust around these cavernous control rooms that rather resembled the engine rooms of transatlantic liners.

But what to do with the building (*Fig. 9*)?

WHAT – YOU MEAN THERE'S MORE?

Fig. 9

One day, out of the blue, I had a phone call in the office from a gentleman with a very strong North African accent asking to meet me to discuss the possibility of his organisation taking on the church.

I offered to come and meet him in his offices, wherever they might be, but he explained that he had no office and no car, so could we meet up at the railway station? This was only five minutes' walk to my own office at Church House, and so I readily agreed.

I waited on the station platform, and at the designated time there descended from the carriage this dark, elegant figure dressed in a long, black cassock, bearing on his head a tall, black, cylindrical hat with no rim and a thick black beard.

I have rarely met such a dignified, courteous man as Father X.

I suggested that we stroll along to my office, but no, he had only half an hour before his next train, and so perhaps we could conduct our conversation in the station waiting room?

He ran his entire enterprise on his mobile phone – quite a rarity in those days. He could not write English and relied on his lay colleagues for the office work. Father X represented the regional episcopate of the Coptic Church of Egypt. He had a large congregation, comprising Egyptian engineers, hospital consultants, lawyers and teachers who had come to England to train, and then decided to remain. (The Coptic Christians in Egypt were tolerated but were prohibited from tertiary education and several professions.) The Coptics were clearly a denomination ruled by clericalism. There was no question of these professional lay members being involved in taking decisions. Father X was the man in charge.

We had a delightful, if stilted, discussion sitting in the semi-darkness of the dank waiting room, our only audience being a drunk, huddled in the far corner, muttering to himself.

Money was no object, and we agreed a set of recommendations to put before our respective authorities. I felt obliged to warn him that a structural survey might be prudent. We politely bowed to one another, and I escorted him to the door of his railway carriage.

I never heard from him, or the Coptic Church, ever again.

In the end, after a year or so, we found a buyer in the Texan branch of the Romanian Orthodox Church. This was run by a very loud and ardent American convert who was a millionaire. Unfortunately, he was also a charlatan, and his charity went bust some years later. The church is now a thriving place of worship with the Greek Orthodox.

The Compton organ sadly lies there unused, gathering dust to the sound of the occasional bell and gong which comprise the sole musical accompaniment to the Orthodox liturgy. As it was regarded by the borough conservation officer as part of the fabric of the listed building, we were prohibited from removing it to a good home elsewhere. What a tragedy for a fine musical instrument.

A less happy story, indeed quite the opposite extreme, is the case of St James, a modest single cell Victorian building in a small and rather remote country village. The church is set in the centre of its graveyard, which is always a tricky feature when an alternative use of the structure becomes necessary. In this, as in so many cases, the building became redundant for church use, but not the burial ground, which remained under parochial control for continued interment of the dead of the parish.

The building was bought by a young and highly strung, gifted musician who converted it sensitively into a workshop for building mechanical pipe organs that played themselves via an ingenious system of rollers and perforated card, much the same as fairground organs but with classical registrations. In a gallery was his accommodation, and he lived there with his male companion.

Most regrettably and disgracefully, the local village community (with one or two rare exceptions) took against this set-up and from the very outset made his life a misery.

They deliberately wandered all over his little garden; undertook activities in the graveyard without giving him the due notice to which he was entitled; completely ostracised him in the village; and started to cause small incidents of criminal damage to his possessions. He naturally complained to the police and to the Church Commissioners and to the civil parish council, the PCC and the vicar, but to no avail. In the end he found in me the only sympathetic ear, and 'a telephone call for you from Ian X' became a frequent precursor to forty minutes on the phone in the office, with me from time to time 'mming' and 'ahhing' as best I could. I think I was the only counsellor he had, poor fellow, but what could I do to alleviate his sufferings?

And then things took a turn for the worse. He wrote to me to report that a local man had assaulted him in the churchyard, hitting him so badly in the face, and damaging his glasses, that he was totally blinded in one eye and partially in the other. I believe an arrest was made and the law took its course, but this did nothing for Ian's mental or physical health, nor for his ability to continue to build his musical instruments that required minute detail and accuracy.

After many years of continued misery, he did manage to sell the property and move into sheltered accommodation elsewhere in the country, a sad end to a not untypical story of 1980's rural antagonisms, prejudices and hate.

Sometimes the issues affecting church property are deliberate, and sometimes they are entirely unintended. An example of the latter concerns a former church in a tiny village that lay at the edge of a large, landed estate, ruled at the time by the rather fierce widow of a more mild scion of the gentry concerned, who had died many years previously.

The church itself (unusual in having no dedication to any Saint) was taken on by the Friends of Friendless Churches, an admirable national charity that 'does what it says on the label'.

In ecclesiastical law, the Church Plate (the chalices, patens and associated crockery, usually of solid silver and of great age) must remain with the local benefice when the church building is otherwise disposed of upon closure. The Plate is normally dispersed to other churches in the benefice, with the result in recent years that every church possesses an ever-accumulating hoard of neglected and half-forgotten silverware tucked away in the church vestry, the parsonage house or anywhere else that has the storage space.

Many years after the church was safely in the hands of the Friends, the elderly dowager in the nearby stately home died, and in due course her executors decided to sell up. The impressive contents of the house were catalogued and put up for auction at the prestigious regional auction house in the cathedral city. Its catalogues are always full of glossy photographs of the almost priceless chattels that often come up for sale, and this one was no exception.

Prominent on an inner page was a photograph and listing for a truly splendid chalice of venerable date, expected to fetch a sum in at least five figures.

This was brought to my attention by a long-standing member of my Redundant Churches Uses Committee who had much expertise in these matters. He had been surprised to see the catalogue entry, knowing that the public sale of such an item was strictly contrary to ecclesiastical law.

I immediately telephoned the senior partner of the auctioneers and explained the reason for our reservations. He promised to look into the provenance of this chalice.

A week later, he phoned me to report what he had discovered. More than twenty-five years earlier, the lady of the house had been churchwarden and had agreed to store one of the many unused chalices in her secure cabinet at home. No one had subsequently given any thought to it. Understandably, when her executor son-in-law turned out the contents of the cabinet, he naturally took it for granted that it all belonged to Mum-in-law's personal estate and entered everything for auction.

The chalice was immediately withdrawn from sale and taken to the other parish church, where no doubt it joined a quantity of similar items in the overcrowded vestry safe.

It does seem a little odd (and therefore entirely consistent with much of the Church of England) that consent to the sale of surplus Church Plate is still an exceptional rarity. Selling the historic family silver is perhaps always a matter of regret, but when one considers the time, energy and resources of church folk in maintaining the fabric of their institution alongside their use of what is left for mission and pastoral ministry, surely the asset value is better released. One would not, of course, wish the facility to be opened up all in one go. The public market would be so awash with ecclesiastical silver that its value would plummet. Much the same happened to the market for church pews in the 1970s.

WHAT – YOU MEAN THERE'S MORE?

Now, back to antagonism and infighting – the staple diet of many church closures.

A small, but affecting, example of what could frequently occur was at the public village meeting called to consult the community at large over a proposal (from the vicar and churchwardens) that the Church of St John the Baptist should be closed. The archdeacon and I attended, representing the diocesan interest.

The regular congregation had dwindled to half a dozen in what was a large village, but the pews that evening were packed solid. Grim, red-faced locals glared at those of us (Archdeacon, Vicar and me) seated facing them at the front.

The churchwardens, incidentally, were nowhere to be seen.

The archdeacon emphasised how close the church was to two others, one indeed in the same parish. The number of services in the parish as a whole would remain the same. Burials would continue as normal in the surrounding churchyard. The three brave members of the congregation actually present did their best to support the proposal in the interests of the mission and ministry of the church in the community, but they were mild mannered, decent folk unused to verbal warfare.

They sat down and the big guns from the secular crowd opened fire, recalling their great-grandparents' weddings and funerals there; the annual Father Christmas bash that they occasionally brought their grandchildren to; the cheek of the churchwardens in kowtowing to the vicar (both were recent incomers); and last but not least the vandalism, perversity, sacrilege and treason of the vicar herself, who should hang her head in shame and resign as quickly as possible.

Well, by this stage people had risen from their pews and were walking about, joining little huddled groups of like-minded opposition, all talking loudly at one another.

The vicar had quietly crept into a corner pew out of the light, with her head in her hands. I got up to sit alongside her in mutual support and realised that she was in tears.

I am not generally in the habit of putting my arm around clergy and giving them a cuddle, but on that occasion, it seemed to me to be justified.

(Which reminds me of the only time I have ever hugged an archdeacon with a kiss on both cheeks. Well, she was rather nice, and it was her farewell party. This was shortly before I retired, and she was going off to be the first female archdeacon in the Church of England. Firsts all round.)

SEVEN

WHAT HAS THE MINISTRY OF DEFENCE GOT TO DO WITH IT?

My redoubtable personal secretary, and secretary to the Diocesan Property Department, had been in the Diocesan Office since leaving college aged seventeen and retired from it aged sixty-five some years after I had left. The prospect of Linda retiring before me was not something I was ever prepared to contemplate.

(It was Linda who probably instilled in my younger daughter Lamorna her expertise in dealing with computer problems. She would prop Lamorna (aged about six) up on a chair with a pile of files and let her explore the office computer to her heart's content.)

Apart from her incredible typing speed – she often had to wait for her electric typewriter to catch up – Linda's tour de force was her uncanny ability to recognise and remember people's voices on the telephone. They only had to clear their throat and she would respond to them by name and promptly switch them through to me fully identified, even if they had not phoned for months.

I could always tell whether such a caller was good news or bad by the tone of voice with which she patched me through. If her voice hid a smile, I knew it was someone I would prefer to have gone to great lengths to avoid. If she did so by mimicking the voice of the caller, it would be a warning signal for me to ask her to respond that I was at present out of the office and unlikely to return for several days, if ever.

One such irritant was an extraordinary woman who lived the life of an opt-out hippie and self-published works of tedious poetry and protest songs she wrote in support of her militant crusade against armaments, nuclear or otherwise, and the works of the armed services in general and in particular. She had inherited her strident pacifism from her father, who had been a prominent local councillor and much respected figure in his long but unsuccessful campaign to keep open the roads and paths through part of the vast acreage occupied by the Ministry of Defence as training grounds and firing ranges.

Right in the centre of this huge expanse of downland, in a shallow valley, lay the remains of an abandoned village whose residents had been forced to leave in 1943 when the area was commandeered for military purposes. Each village tenant had been given a letter which they understood to imply a commitment to return their homes to the residents once hostilities had ceased, a claim that was later officially denied.

WHAT HAS THE MINISTRY OF DEFENCE GOT TO DO WITH IT?

The army had declined any such undertaking, and even forty-five years later, the issue still rankled with many of the local community in the nearest town. Those most vociferous in their continued protest were not so much the few remaining elderly dispossessed of the village but certain individuals who saw this issue as a useful means of promoting themselves within local politics and other spheres of influence.

The parish church on the edge of the village had survived army occupation largely thanks to a gentleman's agreement at the time, that the military authorities would keep the building wind- and watertight. The army honoured this agreement after a fashion, until the turn of the twenty-first century, when it gave notice that responsibility would have to be resumed by the parish. The church and churchyard (and the nearby Baptist burial ground) were the only properties still remaining in their original ownership.

The church was only accessible on very few days in the year, and a resumption of use by the parish, let alone its maintenance and restoration, was of course quite out of the question.

And so, another redundancy fell into my lap, and I had the awkward task of finding someone to take on a building and churchyard that could only be visited infrequently with an army escort. Unsurprisingly, the church had been largely forgotten over the years, but it was an historic structure of considerable interest, adorned with the faded remains of medieval monochrome wall paintings and very early seventeenth-century change-ringing graffiti in the bell-ringing chamber. Now, the church and graveyard, which contained some notable but dilapidated table tombs, suddenly hit the limelight, and English Heritage (as it was then known) promptly listed them Grade I.

This helped me considerably, as the church would now be a strong candidate for vesting in the Churches Conservation Trust, an august national body funded both by the C of E and the government to protect just such buildings in perpetuity. At the time, Frank Field MP was Chairman of the Trust, and he telephoned me one day to say that he was dead against such a vesting, because he believed that visitor numbers would be minimal and access for restoration and maintenance a major problem with the army.

I contacted the army training area commandant to reach an agreement over access. He invited me to a day out with him to discuss the matter. In an army Land Rover, he drove me at great speed all over the acreage of the training area, pointing out the salient features, but particularly the wildlife. The colonel was quite evidently far more interested in the flora and fauna, and notably the bird life, of that wilderness then he was in the army manoeuvres, and I learnt a lot.

At any rate, he was entirely relaxed about access arrangements for building contractors for the church, so my object was achieved.

So far, so good. However, there was competition for the future management of the church which was far less welcome. For some years, there had been a group of local people, including one or two former residents who had been children at the time of their evacuation, who had set themselves up as 'Friends' of the church and had raised funds towards the regular annual pilgrimages to the church and village. This group was presently chaired by a former local town councillor, who had gathered around him a small set of cronies, to the virtual exclusion of others who wished to express a voice. As a result, meetings in the nearby town where the Friends met formally in a pub, tended to be contentious and acrimonious.

The disposition and recording of subscriptions and donations to the Friends were less than transparent, and doubts had been expressed about whose pockets they might be lining.

The leadership of these Friends felt that they had an established right to a major role in the future control of the church, now that the Ministry of Defence had called an end to the gentleman's agreement to maintain the building.

The hippie girl who kept phoning me up and sending me unsolicited and lengthy protest literature drifted in and out of this political scenario, believing that her parental profile justified by inheritance her own right to a voice in the future of the church and village.

I decided to call a meeting. Representatives of my diocesan committee; the regional representative of the Churches Conservation Trust (who was also, thank goodness, a member of my committee and a leading light in the events held in the church); the leadership of the Friends; and three elderly and delightful former residents of the village all turned up in the board room at Church House in the cathedral city, and I invited them in turn to express a view on the future management of the church and churchyard.

Now, I make no claim to the level of skill required by the Speaker of the House of Commons to control rowdy Members of Parliament during divisive debates, but I doubt whether Dame Betty Boothroyd herself could have mastered this motley contingent of competing interests.

After an hour or so, I drew a halt to the proceedings, thanked them all for their valued contributions and staggered home to my family in a limp and wan state that required a generous dram or two of Scotch to restore my faculties to near normal condition.

Suffice it to say that the church was duly vested in the Churches Conservation Trust and has ever since sustained record numbers of annual visitors, more than any other CCT church in England.

*

My other engagement with the Ministry of Defence in this context was far more placid and delightful.

A rather similar scenario had occurred in a tiny feudal village down on the coast. The inhabitants were required to evacuate the area for the US army to rehearse their forthcoming D-Day landings. At the end of the war, the area continued in military use as a firing range for artillery, and the abandoned cottages, mansion house and huge four-square parsonage house gently fell into ruin, albeit with an undertaking that the gunners would refrain from actually using them as targets. This was successful except for a stray shell which went clean through the wall of the little village school (now happily restored and refurnished as one of the visitor attractions).

WHAT HAS THE MINISTRY OF DEFENCE GOT TO DO WITH IT?

The residents, once again, had been led to believe that they could return to their homes after the hostilities had ended.

I think that one should not become too nostalgic for the living conditions of the villagers ejected from their tenancies during the war. Most of those cottages were damp, cold, miles from town shops and lacking mains water, electricity or drainage. Several of the residents, rehoused in spanking-new council houses on the edge of the local town, with all mod cons laid on, would have been most reluctant to return to their old way of life.

The parish church was the only property remaining in pre-war ownership, and it had survived in surprisingly good condition. It stood there in isolated limbo from 1943 to 1977, when the diocese decided to formalise the matter. We leased it to the MoD for twenty-one years, at an annual rent of five pounds, as a 'rest and exhibition centre', on the basis that the army would keep it in good repair and create a local history display inside.

The long-serving Range Officer, Major Mick, took a particular interest in the old village and devoted much energy and money (apocryphally, out of his training budget) into conserving the now roofless structures and presenting them attractively for the growing number of visitors to the village and nearby beach during designated open days.

Following a fire, the parsonage was too damaged to save in its entirety and today stands rather incongruously as a single-storey edifice open to the skies but closed to the public. The church, on the other hand, has been transformed into a most impressive museum and display space for village history, with the chancel preserved in its ecclesiastical form – somewhat enhanced, I would suggest, with Anglo-Catholic colour and decoration that owes more to Major Mick's imagination than to its original style as a modest country kirk.

The major took me on one occasion to the remains of the fascinating old mansion house hidden in woodland further up the valley. This is strictly out of bounds to the public, as it is surrounded by ground littered with unexploded armament shells. He and I were accompanied by a sapper walking ahead of us, swinging a metal detector to and fro over the soil to guide us through unscathed.

EIGHT
SURELY IT WASN'T ALWAYS SUCH FUN?

Abandoned buildings are never much fun. I almost always felt a strong sense of pathos and poignancy when wandering for the first time around a church that had been closed for worship, the last-ever service having been held there a week or so previously, the loyal remnants of a once thriving congregation having picked up their hats and coats, glancing with moist eyes around the decaying furnishings, and quietly closing the old door behind them, never to return (*Fig. 10*).

I would stand there at the west end, having inspected all I needed to inspect, silently absorbing in its own stillness the sanctity and spirituality of the space around me, stone and glass and oak that was saturated with the accumulated prayer and worship of generations of local people. How irrefutable is the doctrine of the Church that once consecrated, no

PARSONAGE AND PARSON

building or object can ever be deconsecrated. That is a spiritual impossibility. Only the administrative and legal consequences of consecration can be brought to a close.

Sad too, in a more materialistic way, was the subsequent visit to a closed church that I would make with the member of my committee who was an expert in recognising and valuing notable works of art, furniture and furnishings. We would draw up a list of chattels and decide our recommendation to the bishop (who became their custodian) as to their disposal.

Fig. 10

It was much like my former experience as a land agent, attending a forced auction sale of farm equipment and farmhouse furniture on the failure or closure of an old agricultural holding, the vendor looking on at the proceedings with a heavy heart and precious memories, with a woebegone expression.

*

My absolute nadir, so far as abandoned buildings were concerned, was in consequence of a tragedy in one of my parsonage houses that even today I find difficult to describe.

SURELY IT WASN'T ALWAYS SUCH FUN?

On the 15th of March 1989 at four o'clock in the morning, an electrical fault (later presumed to have been in the Electricity Board's supply-side equipment at the distribution board under the stairs) set fire to a fine 1930's vicarage. Asleep inside were the vicar and his wife, their four children and two of the children's grandparents who had come for a visit. The fire was raging by the time the family awoke, but the vicar's wife managed to get out and reach a neighbour who was a fireman. He made repeated attempts to reach the children's bedrooms by a ladder but was forced back by the heat and badly burnt.

The three young girls aged eleven, ten and five, lost their lives that night; the rest of the family, including the seven-year-old boy, managed to escape.

I received a phone call at home at breakfast time and drove straight there, persuading a police roadblock some miles away to let me through.

Four fire engines, hoses and exhausted firemen occupied the driveway. Some of the men were sitting on the lawn eating their breakfast. The smoke and steam still obscured the house, but I could immediately see that the roof had completely imploded into the building.

I explained to the district fire officer who I was, and he had to break the news to me of the multiple fatalities. As a father myself of two girls then aged six and three, I felt icy shock. I learned that the bishop and his wife had gathered the remaining family up and later heard that on discharge from hospital, the vicar, his wife and their small son were taken in by the bishop to live in the episcopal house for the time being.

The fire officer asked me to produce the most recent electrical test report on the vicarage installation, and so I rushed off to the office, plucked it from the file and returned to the scene of devastation. Fortunately, the report and its consequent works had all been carried out very recently.

Probably the worst part of my experience was a few days later, when the archdeaconry surveyor and I donned hard hats and made a tour of inspection through the black, dripping, creaking remains of the edifice to determine whether the building was capable of restoration. That decision, in the end, never had to be made because the overwhelming desire of the Church both locally and centrally was for complete clearance of the site. This proved to be long delayed, to much justified criticism, because of continued lengthy investigation by the insurance companies and the electricity authorities, who refused to permit the evidence to be removed for several months.

Two positive and long-lasting initiatives were sparked off by this calamitous incident.

Firstly, until then, the availability and demand for battery-operated smoke detectors in private houses were very limited, but the regional and national press coverage of the tragedy led in a matter of days to a nationwide surge in the market for such devices. Ironmongers and DIY stores could not get enough of them to meet the public clamour. Since then, of course, ceiling-mounted smoke detection in residential buildings has become as basic a provision as mains water.

The second innovation followed a meeting I held with the chief fire officer for the county, who had recently launched a campaign with the big regional house builders, trying to persuade them to adopt a policy that was standard practice in many countries, such as New Zealand, Australia and the USA, which was to install high-pressure sprinkler systems during the construction of new-build dwellings. His initiative was meeting strong resistance from the industry on grounds of cost (and sadly that resistance was never successfully overcome). He asked me if the Church could set an example, which the fire service and the fire prevention industry would publicise on a wide scale, by installing a sprinkler system in every new parsonage house that we built in future.

My Parsonages Committee was enthusiastic, and so we immediately adopted that practice. At the time, in the late 1980s and well into the 1990s, we were building purpose-designed parsonages on a wide scale and became very experienced in these quite complex installations.

Some years later, our policy bore fruit in one of our new houses, a vicarage, in an operation which undoubtedly saved a young life.

The vicar had a small job to do in the garden, and since his wife was out, he put their small toddler son in the utility room and shut the doors. This little boy was very fond of sitting and playing in the dog basket in that room.

Unfortunately, a box of matches had been left on the sink unit, and the child had found it…

The vicar suddenly heard the sprinkler system alarm go off and rushed indoors through the back door, to the utility room. This was awash with water from the overhead sprinkler, and full of steam and smoke, with a very wet toddler crying in the dog basket underneath. The fire was out but had clearly taken hold sufficiently to warp and melt the worktop and badly scorch the wall right up to the ceiling.

The door into the kitchen had been closed and was scorched on the utility side, but only a dribble of water had seeped beneath it into the kitchen which was otherwise entirely unscathed.

All the vicar had to do was turn off the single sprinkler 'trip' switch and mop up the mess on the utility floor.

Almost without doubt, had there been no sprinkler, the child would have died asphyxiated or burnt to death.

NINE
A GOOD PLACE TO WORK?

The Christian Church is often held out by its proponents as the only membership organisation with a raison d'être to serve and benefit non-members. That was undoubtedly the intention of its founder when gathering a motley collection of men and women around him as disciples and carers. Their successors down to the present day, myself included, have become rather less single-minded, having found the Church to be an attractive society in which to belong for its own sake.

This enchantment no doubt varies in degree from one denomination to another, and from one era to the next, but nowhere can it be truer, surely, than in the good old Church of England. This personal record is no place to begin extolling the theology or doctrine of the Church in any depth, but I will say that the breadth of its embrace has developed within it a mellow camaraderie that fully extended, in my experience, to life as a diocesan administrative professional. I could have wished for no other career.

There were, of course, individuals, both ordained and lay, with whom I had to 'cope', but, overwhelmingly, my relationship with those whose homes were in my care – juggling need with little money – was heart-warming and privileged.

Especially in the early years – long before the time of personal computers, email, Internet or social media, when communication beyond the home was by Royal Mail post or GPO telephones – what I found in parsonage houses was loneliness. Many of my days were spent with elbows on the kitchen table of one vicarage or another, called there on the pretext of some administrative or practical management issue but ending up with a simple listening ear to the woes and worries of isolated people whose role in their community inhibited any such discourse with those around them locally.

With parish laity – churchwardens, treasurers and others – there was always a tension between 'them and us'; those bureaucrats at the diocese and us folk in the parish doing all the work and raising all the money. That antipathy has probably diminished in recent years, as representative bodies in society have become less formalised and stereotyped.

In my dealings with parish clergy, however, I was prevailingly rewarded with the warmth of appreciation and gratitude. In how many other spheres of employment could one expect to hear that depiction of one's clients?

A GOOD PLACE TO WORK?

Their eccentricity is a joy to remember, but my professional association and fellowship with so many dear souls who comprise our Church of England is a delight that will remain an indelible memory.

ACKNOWLEDGEMENTS

I am grateful to Robert Macdonald, whose offer to include a contribution from me in an article he was penning for the newsletter of The Rectory Society motivated me to keep on writing.

As memories flooded back, they were accompanied by warm thoughts of particular former colleagues without whom my ecclesiastical reminiscences would have been barren indeed. To list them all would take another book, and so I commemorate here the names only of those who are sadly no longer with us: Christopher Ross, John Voaden, Canon Richard Askew, the Ven Ted Ward, the Ven Dick Sharp, the Ven John Smith, the Ven Geoff Walton, George Hobbs, Ron Jones, Jeffrey Ashenden, Barbara Chapman, Douglas Stewart, Chris Love, Dacre Stroud and, of course, my dedicatee Bishop John Neale.

I ought also to be grateful to the partners of Strutt & Parker who made me redundant as a very junior agricultural land agent in 1980, necessarily prompting a career with the Church of England that proved both fulfilling and fun.

This book was written in biro on long absences aboard my boat. For this I am indebted to my wife Biddy for her patience and forbearance and to Lalla Hitchings for converting sodden sheets of paper into intelligible script.

As ever, my thanks are extended to all at The Book Guild for their unfailing courtesy and guidance, especially my copy editor Lauren Stenning.